W9-AUT-012

SCIENTOLOGY®

A NEW SLANT ON LIFE

L. Ron Hubbard

BRIDGE PUBLICATIONS, INC.

Published by
Bridge Publications, Inc.
1414 North Catalina Street
Los Angeles, California 90027

Reprinted October 1982
Copyright © 1965, 1972.
by L. Ron Hubbard
ALL RIGHTS RESERVED

ISBN 0-88404-123-9

This book is part of the works of L. Ron Hubbard, who developed
Scientology Applied Religious Philosophy. It is presented to the reader as
a record of observations and research into the nature of the human mind
and spirit, and not as a statement of claims made by the author. The
benefits and goals of Scientology can be attained only by the dedicated
efforts of the reader.

The Hubbard Electrometer, or E-Meter, is a device which is sometimes
used in Scientology. In itself, the E-Meter does nothing. It is not intended or effective for the diagnosis, treatment or prevention of any
disease, or for the improvement of health or any bodily function.

Printed in the United States of America

DIANETICS™: From the Greek *dia* (through) and *nous* (soul), thus "through the soul;" a system for the analysis, control and development of human thought which also provides techniques for increased ability, rationality, and freedom from the discovered single source of aberrations and psychosomatic ills. Introduced May, 1950, with publication of *Dianetics: The Modern Science of Mental Health* by L. Ron Hubbard. Dianetics is what the soul is doing to the body.

SCIENTOLOGY® is an applied religious philosophy and technology resolving problems of spirit, life and thought; discovered, developed and organized by L. Ron Hubbard as a result of his earlier Dianetic discoveries. Coming from the Latin, *scio* (knowing) and the Greek *logos* (study), Scientology means "knowing how to know" or "the study of wisdom." Scientology is the study and handling of the spirit in relationship to itself, universes and other life.

You can always write to Ron:

I am always willing to help. By my own creed, a being is only as valuable as he can serve others.

Any message addressed to me and sent to the address of the nearest organization listed in the back of this book shall be given prompt and full attention in accordance with my wishes.

CONTENTS

*"The human mind
is capable of resolving the problem
of the human mind."* — L.R.H.

IMPORTANT NOTE

In studying this book be very, very certain you never go past a word you do not fully understand.

The only reason a person gives up a study or becomes confused or unable to learn is that he or she has gone past a word or phrase that was not understood.

If the material becomes confusing or you can't seem to grasp it, there will be a word just earlier that you have not understood. Don't go any further, but go back to BEFORE you got into trouble, find the misunderstood word and get it defined.

IS IT POSSIBLE TO BE HAPPY?

Is it possible to be happy?

A great many people wonder whether half of us even *exist* in this modern, rushing world. Very often an individual can have a million dollars, he can have everything his heart apparently desires, and is still unhappy. We take the case of somebody who has worked all his life; he has worked hard and he has raised a big family. He has looked forward to that time in his life when he, at last, can retire and be happy and be cheerful, and have lots of time to do all the things he has wanted to do; and then we see him after he has retired—and is he happy? No. He's sitting there thinking about the good old days when he was working hard.

Our main problem in life is happiness, but I'll tell you more in a moment. The world may or may not be designed to be a happy one. It may not be possible for you to be happy in this world, and yet nearly all of us have a goal to be happy and cheerful about existence.

You know, very often we look at the world around us and say that nobody could be happy in this place. We look at the dirty dishes in the sink, and the car needing a coat of paint, and at the fact that we need a new gas heater, we need a new coat, we need new shoes or we would just like to have better shoes; and so, how could anyone possibly be happy when actually he can't have everything he wants. He is unable to do all the things he'd like to do, and therefore, this environment doesn't permit a person to be as happy as he could be. Well, I'll tell you a funny thing—a lot of philosophers have said this many, many times—but the truth of the matter is that all the happiness *you* ever find lies in *you*.

You remember when you were maybe five years old, and you went out in the morning and you looked at the day, and it was a very, very beautiful day, and you looked at the flowers, and they were *very* beautiful flowers; twenty-five years later you get up in the morning, you take a look at the flowers—they are wilted. The day isn't a happy day. Well, what has changed? You know they are the same flowers, it's the same world, something must have changed. Probably it was you.

Actually a little child derives all of his "how" of life from the grace he puts upon life. He waves a magic hand and brings all manner of interesting things into being out in the society. Here is this big, strong brute of a man riding his iron steed, up and down, and boy, he'd like to be a cop. Yes sir! He would sure like to be a cop; and twenty-five years later he looks at that cop riding up and down and checks his speedometer and says, "Doggone these cops!"

Well, what is changed here? Has the cop changed? No. Just the attitude *toward* him. One's attitude toward life makes every possible difference in one's living. You know you don't have to study a thousand ancient books to discover that fact. But sometimes it needs to be pointed out again that *life* doesn't change so much as *you*.

Once upon a time, perhaps, you were thinking of being married and having a nice home, and having a nice family; everything would be just fine. The husband would come home and you would put the dinner on the table and everybody would be happy about the whole thing; and then you got married and maybe it didn't quite work out. Somehow or other, he comes home late and he has had an argument with the boss, and he doesn't feel well. He doesn't want to go to the movies, and he doesn't see how you have any work to do anyhow—after all, you sit home all day and do nothing—and you know he doesn't do any work either. He disappears out of the house.

11

He's gone. Then he comes back later in the evening, and quite an argument could ensue over this. Actually, both of you work quite hard. Well, what do we do with a condition like this? Do we just break up the marriage? Or touch a match to the whole house? Or throw the kids in the garbage can? Or go home to mother? Or what do we do?

Well, there are many, many things we could do, and the least of them is to take a look at the environment. You know, just look around and say, "Where am I? What am I doing here?" And then, once you have found out where you are, why, try to find out how you can make that a little more habitable. The day when you stop building your own environment, when you stop building your own surroundings, when you stop waving a magic hand and gracing everything around you with magic and beauty, things cease to be magical, things cease to be beautiful.

Other people seek happiness in various ways. They seek it hectically, as though it's some sort of mechanism that exists—maybe it's a little machine, maybe it's parked in the cupboard, maybe happiness is down at the next corner, or maybe it's someplace else. They're looking for something, but the odd part of it is, the only time they ever find something is when they put it there first. Now, this doesn't sound very plausible, but it's quite true. Those people who have become unhappy about life *are* unhappy about life solely and completely because life has ceased to be made by them. Here we have the single difference in a human being. We have here a human being who is unhappy, miserable, and isn't getting along in life, who is sick, who doesn't see brightness. Life is handling, running, changing, making him.

And here you have somebody who is happy, who is cheerful, who is strong, who finds that most things are pleasurable; and what do we discover in this person? We find out that he is making life, and there is actually a single difference: are *you* making life or is life making *you?*

Carefully go into this, and you will find out that a person has stopped making life because he himself has decided that life cannot be made. Some failure, some small failure, maybe not graduating with the same class, or maybe that failure that had to do with not marrying quite the first man or woman that came along who seemed desirable, or maybe the failure of having lost a car, or just some minor thing in life started this attitude. A person looked around one day and said, "Well, I've lost," and after that, life makes him; he doesn't make life any more.

Now this would be a very critical situation if

13

nothing could be done about it, but the fact of the matter is that it is the easiest problem of all the problems man faces—changing himself and changing the attitudes of those around him. It is very, very easy to change somebody else's attitude. Yet you are totally dependent upon other people's attitudes—somebody's attitude toward you may make or break your life. Did it ever occur to you that your home holds together because of the attitude the other person has toward you? So there are really two problems here—you would have to change two attitudes. One: your attitude toward somebody else, and two: their attitude toward you. Well, are there ways to do this? Yes, fortunately, there are.

For many, many centuries, Man has desired to know how to change the mind and condition of himself and his fellows. Actually, Man had a cumulative inclination to do this up to relatively few years ago. But, we are making it a very fast paced world; we are making it a world where magic is liable to occur at any time, and has.

Man now understands a great many things about the universe he lives in, which he never understood before. Amongst the things he now understands is the human mind. The human mind is not an unsolved problem. Nineteenth century psychology didn't solve the problem, but that doesn't mean it

14

has not been solved.

In modern times the most interesting miracles are taking place all across this country and across other continents of earth. What do these miracles consist of? They consist of people becoming well when they were ill, incurably ill. They consist of people who were unhappy becoming happy once more. They consist of abolishing the danger inherent in many of the illnesses and many of the conditions of Man. Yet the answer has been with Man all the time; Man has been able to reach out and find this answer, so perhaps Man himself had to change. Perhaps he had to come up to modern times to find out that the physical universe was not composed of demons and ghosts. To outlive his superstitions, to outlive the ignorance of his forbears. Perhaps he had to do everything, including inventing the atom bomb, before he could finally find himself.

Well, he has pretty well mastered the physical universe now. The physical universe is to him no longer a problem, he can do many things with it; and having conquered that, he can now conquer himself. The truth of the matter is he *has* conquered himself. The science of Scientology came about because of a man's increased knowledge of energy. Man became possessed of more information about energy than he had had before in all of his history; and amongst

15

that, he came into possession of information about the energy which is his own mind. The body *is* an energy mechanism. Naturally, a person who cannot handle energy could not handle a body. He would be tired, he would be upset, he would be unhappy, and he looks all around him to find nothing but energy. If he knew a great deal about energy, particularly the energy of himself and the space which surrounds him, he, of course, would know himself; and that, in the final essence, has been his goal for many thousands of years. To know himself.

Scientology has made it possible for him to do so.

THE TRUE STORY OF SCIENTOLOGY

The true story of Scientology is simple, concise and direct. It is quickly told:

1. A philosopher develops a philosophy about life and death;
2. People find it interesting;
3. People find it works;
4. People pass it along to others;
5. It grows.

When we examine this extremely accurate and very brief account, we see that there must be in our civilization some very disturbing elements for anything else to be believed about Scientology.

These disturbing elements are the Merchants of Chaos. They deal in confusion and upset. Their daily bread is made by creating chaos. If chaos were to lessen, so would their incomes.

The politician, the reporter, the psychiatrist with his electric shock machine, the drug manufacturer, the militarist and arms manufacturer, the police and the undertaker, to name the leaders of the list, fatten only upon "the dangerous environment". Even individuals and family members can be Merchants of Chaos.

It is to their interest to make the environment seem as threatening as possible, for only then can they profit. Their incomes, force, and power rise in direct ratio to the amount of threat they can inject into the surroundings of the people. With that threat they can extort revenue, appropriations, heightened circulations and recompense without question. These are the Merchants of Chaos. If they did not generate it and buy and sell it, they would, they suppose, be poor.

For instance, we speak loosely of "good press". Is there any such thing today? Look over a newspaper. Is there anything *good* on the front page? Rather, there is murder and sudden death, disagreement and catastrophe. And even that, bad as it is, is sensationalized to make it seem worse.

This is the cold blooded manufacture of "a dangerous environment". People do not need this news; and if they did, they need the facts, not the upset. But if you hit a person hard enough, he can be made to give up money. That's the basic formula of extortion. That's the way papers are sold. The impact makes them stick.

A paper has to have chaos and confusion. A "news story" has to have "conflict", they say. So there is no good press. There is only bad press about everything. To yearn for "good press" is foolhardy in a society where the Merchants of Chaos reign.

Look what has to be done to the true story of Scientology in order to "make it a news story" by modern press standards. Conflict must be injected where there is none. Therefore, the press has to dream up upset and conflict.

Let us take the first line. How does one make conflict out of it? No. 1, *A philosopher develops a philosophy about life and death.*

The Chaos Merchant has to inject one of several possible conflicts here: He is not a doctor of philosophy, they have to assert. They are never quite bold enough to say it is not a philosophy. But they can and do go on endlessly, as their purpose compels them, in an effort to invalidate the identity of the person developing it.

In actual fact, the developer of the philosophy was very well grounded in academic subjects and the humanities, probably better grounded in formal

19

philosophy alone than teachers of philosophy in universities.

The one man effort is incredible in terms of study and research hours and is a record never approached in living memory, but this would not be considered newsworthy. To write the simple fact that a philosopher had developed a philosophy is not newspaper-type news and it would not disturb the environment. Hence, the elaborate news fictions about No. 1 above.

Then take the second part of the true story. *People find it interesting.* It would be very odd if they didn't, as everyone asks these questions of himself and looks for the answers to his own beingness; and the basic truth of the answers is observable in the conclusions of Scientology.

However, to make this "news" it has to be made disturbing. People are painted as kidnapped or hypnotized and dragged as unwilling victims up to read the books or listen.

The Chaos Merchant leaves No. 3 very thoroughly alone. It is dangerous ground for him. *People find it works.* No hint of workability would ever be attached to Scientology by the press, although there is no doubt in the press mind that it does work.

That's why it's dangerous. It calms the environment. So any time spent trying to convince press that Scientology works is time spent upsetting a reporter.

On No. 4, *People pass it along to others,* the press feels betrayed. "Nobody should believe anything they don't read in the papers. How dare word of mouth exist?" So, to try to stop people from listening, the Chaos Merchant has to use words like "cult". That's "a closed group", whereas Scientology is the most open group on Earth to anyone. And they have to attack organizations and their people to try to keep people out of Scientology.

Now, as for No. 5, *It grows,* we have the true objection.

As truth goes forward, lies die. The slaughter of lies is an act that takes bread from the mouth of a Chaos Merchant. Unless he can lie with wild abandon about "how bad it all is", he thinks he will starve.

The world simply must *not* be a better place, according to the Chaos Merchant. If people were less disturbed, less beaten down by their environment, there would be no new appropriations for police and armies and big rockets, and there'd be not even pennies for a screaming, sensational press.

21

So long as politicians move upward on scandal, police get more pay for more crime, medicos get fatter on more sickness, there will be Merchants of Chaos. They're paid for it.

And their threat is the simple story of Scientology. For that is the true story. And behind its progress, there is a calmer environment in which a man can live and feel better. If you don't believe it, just stop reading newspapers for two weeks, and see if you feel better. Suppose you had all such disturbances handled?

The pity of it is, of course, that even the Merchant of Chaos needs us, not to get fatter, but just to live himself as a being.

So the true story of Scientology is a simple story.

And too true to be turned aside.

TWO RULES FOR HAPPY LIVING

1.   *Be able to experience anything.*
2.   *Cause only those things which others can experience easily.*

Man has had many golden rules. The Buddhist rule of "Do unto others as you would have these others do unto you" has been repeated often in other religions. But such golden rules, while they served to advance man above the animal, resulted in no sure sanity, success, or happiness. Such a golden rule gives only the cause point* or at best, the reflexive effect point**. This is a self-done-to-self thing, and tends to put all on obsessive cause. It gives no thought to what one does about the things done to one by others not so indoctrinated.

How does one handle the evil things done to him?

---

*cause point. Source point, or point of emanation or causation, i.e., in communication, the one who is communicating is the cause point of the communication, and the one who is communicated to is the effect point or receipt point.

**reflexive effect point. A cause point which originates an action calculated to result in an effect on itself.

It is not told in the Buddhist rule. Many random answers resulted. Amongst them are the answers of Christian Science (effects on self don't exist), the answers of early Christians (become a martyr), the answers of Christian ministers (condemn all sin). Such answers to effects created on one bring about a somewhat less than sane state of mind—to say nothing of unhappiness.

After one's house has burned down and the family cremated, it is no great consolation to (1) pretend it didn't happen, (2) liken oneself to Job, or (3) condemn all arsonists.

So long as one fears or suffers from the effect of violence, one will have violence against him. When one *can* experience exactly what is being done to one, ah, magic—it does not happen!

How to be happy in this universe is a problem few prophets or sages have dared to contemplate directly. We find them "handling" the problem of happiness by assuring us that man is doomed to suffering. They seek not to tell us how to be happy, but how to endure being unhappy. Such casual assumption of the impossibility of happiness has led us to ignore any real examination of ways to be happy. Thus, we have floundered forward toward a negative goal—get rid of all the unhappiness on Earth and one would have a liveable Earth. If one seeks to get rid of something continually, one admits continually that he cannot confront it—and thus everyone went down hill. Life became a dwindling spiral of *more* things we could not confront. And thus, we went toward blindness and unhappiness.

To be happy, one must be *able* to confront, which is to say, experience, those things that are.

Unhappiness is only this: the inability to confront that which is.

Hence, (1) *Be able to experience anything.*

The effect side of life deserves great consideration. The self-caused side also deserves examination.

To create only those effects which others could easily experience gives us a clean new rule of living. For, if one does this, then what might he do that he must withhold from others? There is no reason to withhold his own actions or regret them (same thing), if one's own actions are easily experienced by others.

This is a sweeping test (and definition) of good conduct—to do only those things which others can experience.

If you examine your life, you will find you are bothered only by those actions a person did which others were not able to receive. Hence, a person's life can become a hodge-podge of violence ·withheld, which pulls in, then, the violence others caused.

The more actions a person emanated which could not be experienced by others, the worse a person's life became. Recognizing that he was bad cause or that there were too many bad causes already, a person ceased causing things—an unhappy state of being.

Pain, misemotion*, unconsciousness, insanity, all result from causing things others could not experience easily. The reach-withhold phenomenon is the basis of all these things. When one sought to reach in such a way as to make it impossible for another to experience, one did not reach, then, did he? To "reach" with a gun against a person who is unwilling to be shot is not to reach the person, but a protest. All *bad* reaches never reached. So there was no communication, and the end result was a withhold by the person reaching. This reach-withhold became at last, an inability to reach—therefore, low communication, low reality, low affinity. Communication is

*misemotion. Irrational emotion, which is inappropriate to present time environment or situation.

one means of reaching others. So, if one is unable to reach, one's ability to communicate will be low; and one's reality will be low, because if one is unable to communicate, he won't really get to know about others; and with knowing little or nothing about others, one doesn't have any feeling about them either, thus one's affinity will be low. Affinity, reality and communication work together; and if one of these three is high, the other two will be also; but if one is low, so will the others be low.

All bad acts, then, are those acts which cannot be easily experienced at the target end.

On this definition, let us review our own "bad acts". Which ones were bad? Only those that could not be easily experienced by another were bad. Thus, which of society's favorite bad acts are bad? Acts of real violence resulting in pain, unconsciousness, insanity and heavy loss could, at this time, be considered bad. Well, what other acts of yours do you consider "bad"? The things which you have done which you could not easily, yourself, experience, were bad. But the things which you have done which you, yourself, could have experienced, had they been done to you, were *not* bad. That certainly changes one's view of things!

There is no need to lead a violent life just to prove

one can experience. The idea is not to *prove* one can experience, but to regain the *ability* to experience.

Thus, today, we have two golden rules for happiness:

1. Be able to experience anything; and
2. Cause only those things which others are able to experience easily.

Your reaction to these tells you how far you have yet to go.

And if you achieve these two golden rules, you would be one of the happiest and most successful people in this universe, for who could rule you with evil?

WHAT IS THE BASIC MYSTERY?

In the general study of the world and its affairs, we find out that the only way you can make a slave—as if anybody would want one—would be to develop a tremendous amount of mystery about what it's all about and then develop an overwhelming charge* on the mystery line. Not only develop a mystery, but then sell it real good; sell some bogus answer to the mystery.

Man is so used to this that, when you come along and put a perfectly good answer in his hands, why, he drops it like a hot potato, because he knows what all answers are: All answers are carefully derived from mysteries with bogus answers, and all mysteries are going to cost you something sooner or later.

The development of the mystery itself stems from interpersonal relationships and Man's general conflict with his fellows and his environment, and so on. And the basic mystery is—who is he? There's no more basic mystery than that—"who is that fellow

*charge. Emotional charge or energy.

over there?" That is the beginning of individuation, of, not individualism, but individuation, of pulling back from everybody and saying, "I am me and they are 'them', and God knows what they're up to!" And then, after a while, the fellow takes it out of the realm of near blasphemy and puts it into worship. And he says, "Well, God knows what they're up to and he will protect me."

So what do we basically have? We basically have a mystery on who the other fellow is. Now "science" originally meant *truth,* and now it means research revenue. Science has so far abandoned the basic mystery, that they think there's a mystery on what is a floor, what is a ceiling, what is space. That is really a very cooked-up mystery—because that floor and that ceiling and that space is what thee and me agreed to put there, and that's about all it is.

Wherever we have a mystery, we normally have had a disagreement or a misunderstanding or an out-of-communication-ness. And that's all there actually is to it, basically. A fellow had to disagree with whom he was looking at. He knew about it originally and he didn't want to know who that fellow was over there. He didn't want to know anything about the situation, because he had learned a lesson: If he communicated with it, he would be proved wrong!

So we had some people in our midst—you amongst them—who would put up a "this" and say it was a "that". And then you would get these things twisted somehow or another, and you'd say, "Why don't you communicate with *this*?" and then say, "You communicated with *that*." After a while a fellow says, "Aw, I don't want to communicate with either one of them. Dickens with it. Who cares what those things are—I don't want to know." And after that, he'd had it. He said, "I don't want to know," and therefore he had a mystery sitting across from him someplace. And he went so far along this line of not wanting to know that after a while he conceived that he didn't know. And then he went from there and said it's impossible to know.

Wherever Man finds himself deeply instilled, engrossed, surrounded with mystery, he is actually in conflict with himself and himself alone. That is why processing* works. THE ONLY ABERRATION** IS DENIAL OF SELF. Nobody else can do anything to *you*, but YOU. That is a horrible state of affairs. You can do something to you, but it requires

---

*processing. The application of Scientology technology to an individual toward the end of helping that individual find out things about himself. This application is done by an Auditor (means one who listens); and the technology of the application, as well as the technology that is applied, is very precise.
**aberration. Any departure from rationality.

31

your postulate*, your agreement or your disagreement, before anything can happen to you. People have to agree to be ill; they have to agree to be stupid; they have to agree to be in mystery.

People are the victims of their own flinch. They are the victims of their own postulates, the victims of their own belief that they are inadequate.

An individual has to postulate into existence his own aberration, his own flinch, his own stupidity, his own lack of confidence, and his own bad luck.

---

*postulate. A conclusion, decision or resolution made by the individual himself.

MAN'S SEARCH FOR HIS SOUL

For countless ages past, Man has been engaged upon a search.

All thinkers in all ages have contributed their opinion and considerations to it. No scientist, no philosopher, no leader has failed to comment upon it. Billions of men have died for one opinion or another on the subject of this search and no civilization, mighty or poor, in ancient or in modern times has endured without battle on its account.

The human soul, to the civilized and barbaric alike, has been an endless source of interest, attention, hate or adoration.

To say that I have found the answer to all riddles of the soul would be inaccurate and presumptuous. To discount what I have come to know and to fail to make that known after observing its benefits would be a sin of omission against Man.

After thirty-one years of inquiry and thought and after fifteen years of public activity wherein I observed the material at work and its results, I can announce that, in the knowledge I have developed, there must lie the answer to that riddle, to that enigma, to that problem—the human soul—for under my hands and others, I have seen the best in Man rehabilitated.

From the time since I first made a theta clear*, I have been, with some reluctance, out beyond any realm of the scientific known; and now that I have myself cleared half a hundred, and auditors** I have trained, many times that, I must face the fact that we have reached that merger point where science and religion meet, and we must now cease to pretend to deal with material goals alone.

We cannot deal in the realm of the human soul and ignore the fact. Man has too long pursued this search

*theta clear. An individual who in Scientology processing has attained the certainty of his identity as a being apart from that of the body. The terms clear, clearing, etc. originally came into use by analogy to an adding machine. If some numbers are held down in the machine, then in adding a column of figures one arrives at wrong answers. If the held-down numbers are then *cleared,* one arrives at correct answers. Aberration is likened to the held-down numbers; hence the term "clearing", and a Scientology clear is one who has been cleared of aberrations and has attained an extremely high level of spiritual freedom and ability.
**auditor. One who applies Scientology technology to another individual. Auditor means one who listens.

for its happy culmination here to be muffled by vague and scientific terms.

Religion, not science, has carried this search, this war, through the millenia. Science has all but swallowed Man with an ideology which denies the soul, a symptom of the failure of science in that search.

One cannot now play traitor to the Men of God who sought, these ages past, to bring Man from the darkness.

We, in Scientology, belong in the ranks of the seekers after truth, not in the rearguard of the makers of the atom bomb.

However, science too, has had its role in these endeavors; and nuclear physics, whatever crime it does against Man, may yet be redeemed by having been of aid in finding for Man the soul of which science had all but deprived him.

No Auditor can easily close his eyes to the results he achieves today or fail to see them superior to the materialistic technologies he earlier used. For we can know, with all else we know, that the human soul, freed, is the only effective therapeutic agent we have. But our goals, no matter our miracles with bodies today, exceed physical health and better men.

Scientology is the science of knowing how to know. It has taught us that a man IS his own immortal soul. And it gives us little choice, but to announce to a world, no matter how it receives it, that nuclear physics and religion have joined hands and that we in Scientology perform those miracles for which Man, through all his search, has hoped.

The individual may hate God or despise priests. He cannot ignore, however, the evidence that he is his own soul. Thus we have resolved our riddle and found the answer simple.

THE REASON WHY

Life can best be understood by likening it to a game. Since we are exterior to a great number of games, we can regard them with a detached eye. If we were exterior to Life instead of being involved and immersed in the living of it, it would look to us much like games look to us from our present vantage point.

Despite the amount of suffering, pain, misery, sorrow and travail which can exist in life, the reason for existence is the same reason as one has to play a game—interest, contest, activity and possession. The truth of this assertion is established by an observation of the elements of games and then applying these elements to life itself. When we do this we find nothing left wanting in the panorama of life.

By game we mean a contest of person against person or team against team. When we say games we mean such games as baseball, polo, chess or any other such pastime. It may at one time have struck you as peculiar that men would risk bodily injury in the field of play just for the sake of "amusement". So it might strike you as peculiar that people would go on living or would enter into the "game of life" at the risk of all the sorrow, travail and pain just to have something to do. Evidently there is no greater curse than total idleness. Of course there is that condition where a person continues to play a game in which he is no longer interested.

If you will but look about the room and check off items in which you are not interested, you will discover something remarkable. In a short time you will find that there is nothing in the room in which you are not interested. You are interested in everything. However, disinterest itself is one of the mechanisms of play. In order to hide something it is only necessary to make everyone disinterested in the place where the item is hidden. Disinterest is not an immediate result of interest which has worn out. Disinterest is a commodity in itself. It is palpable, it exists.

By studying the elements (factors) of games (contests) we find ourselves in possession of the elements of life.

Life is a game. A game consists of *freedom, barriers* and *purposes.* This is a scientific fact, not merely an observation.

Freedom exists amongst barriers. A totality of

barriers and a totality of freedom alike are no-game conditions. Each is similarly cruel. Each is similarly purposeless.

Great revolutionary movements fail. They promise unlimited freedom. That is the road to failure. Only stupid visionaries chant of endless freedom. Only the afraid and the ignorant speak of and insist upon unlimited barriers.

When the relation between freedom and barriers becomes too unbalanced, an unhappiness results.

"Freedom from" is all right only so long as there is a place to be free *to*. An endless desire for *freedom from* is a perfect trap, a fear of all things.

Barriers are composed of inhibiting (limiting) ideas, space, energy, masses and time. Freedom in its entirety would be a total absence of these things—but it would also be a freedom without thought or action, an unhappy condition of total nothingness.

Fixed on too many barriers, man yearns to be free. But launched suddenly into total freedom he is purposeless and miserable. He needs a gradient.

There is *freedom* amongst barriers. If the barriers

are known and the freedoms are known there can be life, living, happiness a game.

The restrictions of a government, or a job, give an employee his freedom. Without known restrictions, an employee is a slave, doomed to the fears of uncertainty in all his actions.

Executives in business and government can fail in three ways and, thus, bring about a chaos in their department. They can:
1. seem to give endless freedom;
2. seem to give endless barriers;
3. make neither freedom nor barriers certain.

Executive competence, therefore, consists of imposing and enforcing an adequate balance between their people's freedom and the unit's barriers and in being precise and consistent about those freedoms and barriers. Such an executive, adding only in himself initiative and purpose, can have a department with initiative and purpose.

An employee, buying and/or insisting upon freedom only, will become a slave. Knowing the above facts, he must insist upon a workable balance between freedom and barriers.

There are various states of mind which bring

40

about happiness. That state of mind which insists only upon freedom can bring about nothing but unhappiness. It would be better to develop a thought pattern which looked for new ways to be entrapped and things to be trapped in, than to suffer the eventual total entrapment of dwelling upon freedom only. A man who is willing to accept restrictions and barriers and is not afraid of them is free. A man who does nothing but fight restrictions and barriers will usually be trapped.

As it can be seen in any game, purposes become counterposed. There is a matter of purpose-counter-purpose in almost any game played in a field with two teams. One team has the idea of reaching the goal of the other, and the other has the idea of reaching the goal of the first. Their purposes are at war, and this warring of purposes makes a game.

The war of purposes gives us what we call problems. A problem consists of two or more purposes opposed. It does not matter what problem you face or have faced, the basic anatomy of that problem is purpose-counter-purpose.

In actual testing in Scientology, it has been discovered that a person begins to suffer from problems when he does not have enough of them. There is the old saw (maxim) that, if you want a thing done, give it to a busy man to do. Similarly, if you want a happy associate, make sure that he is a man who can have lots of problems.

We have the oddity of a high incidence of neurosis in the families of the rich. These people have very little to do and have very few problems. The basic problems of food, clothing and shelter are already solved for them. We would suppose then, if it were true that an individual's happiness depended only upon his freedom, these people would be happy. However, they are not happy. What brings about their unhappiness? It is the lack of problems.

An unhappy man is one who is considering continually how to become free. One sees this in the clerk who is continually trying to avoid work. Although he has a great deal of leisure time, he is not enjoying any part of it. He is trying to avoid contact with people, objects, energies and spaces. He eventually becomes trapped in a sort of lethargy. If this man could merely change his mind and start "worrying" about how he could get more work to do, his happiness level would increase markedly. One who is plotting continually how to get out of things will be miserable. One who is plotting how to get into things has a much better chance of becoming happy.

42

There is, of course, the matter of being forced to play games in which one has no interest—a war into which one is drafted is an excellent example of this. One is not interested in the purposes of the war and yet one finds himself fighting it. Thus there must be an additional element and this element is "the power of choice".

One could say then that life is a game and that the ability to play a game consists of tolerance for freedom and barriers and an insight into purposes with the power of choice over participation.

These four elements, freedom, barriers, purposes and power of choice, are the guiding elements of life. There are only two factors above these and both of them are related to these. The first is the ability to create, with of course its negative, the ability to uncreate, and the second is the ability to make a postulate (to consider, to say a thing and have it be true). This, then, is the broad picture of life, and these elements are used in its understanding, in bringing life into focus and in making it less confusing.

WHAT IS KNOWLEDGE?

Knowledge is certainty; knowledge is *not* data. Knowingness itself is certainty. Sanity is certainty, providing only that that certainty does not fall beyond the conviction of another when he views it.

To obtain a certainty one must be able to observe. But what is the level of certainty required? And what is the level of observation required for a certainty or a knowledge to exist?

If a man can stand before a tree and by sight, touch or other perception know that he is confronting a tree and be able to perceive its form and be quite sure he is confronting a tree, we have the level of certainty required. If the man will not look at the tree or, although it is observably a tree to others, if he discovers it to be a blade of grass or a sun, then he is below the level of certainty required. Some other person helpfully inclined would have to direct his perception to the tree until the man perceived without duress that it was indeed a tree he confronted. That is the only level of certainty required in order to qualify knowledge, for knowledge is observation and is given to those who would look.

In order to obtain knowledge and certainty, it is necessary to be able to observe, in fact, three universes in which there could be trees. The first of these is one's own universe; one should be able to create for his own observation in its total form for total perception, a tree. The second universe would be the material universe, which is the universe of matter, energy, space and time and is the common meeting ground of all of us. The third universe is actually a class of universes, which could be called "the other fellow's universe", for he and all the class of "other fellows" have universes of their own.

A doctor, for instance, may seem entirely certain of the cause of some disease, yet it depends upon the doctor's certainty for the layman to accept that cause of the disease. That penicillin cures certain things is a certainty to the doctor even when penicillin suddenly and inexplicably fails to cure something. Any inexplicable failure introduces an uncertainty, which thereafter removes the subject from the realm of an easily obtained certainty.

We have here, then, a parallel between certainty and sanity.

The less certain the individual on any subject, the less sane he could be said to be upon that subject; the less certain he is of what he views in the material universe, what he views in his own or the other fellow's universe, the less sane he could be said to be.

The road to sanity is demonstrably the road to increasing certainty. Starting at any level, it is only necessary to obtain a fair degree of certainty on the material universe to improve considerably one's beingness. Above that, one obtains some certainty of his own universe and some certainty of the other fellow's universe.

Certainty, then, is clarity of observation. Of course, above this, vitally so, is certainty in creation. Here is the artist, here is the master, here is the very great spirit.

As one advances he discovers that what he first perceived as a certainty can be considerably improved. Thus we have certainty as a gradient scale*. It is not an absolute, but it is defined as the certainty

*gradient scale. A scale of advancing little by little or in easy stages toward something—a scale of graduals, i.e., between black and white there are many shades of gray, the ones at the white end being very light, but advancing in darkness until they are very dark gray, and then black. Even with the black and the white, one can always find a deeper black or a whiter white, so neither of them are absolutely black or absolutely white.

46

that one perceives or the certainty that one creates what one perceives or the certainty that there is perception. Sanity and perception, certainty and perception, knowledge and observation, are then all of a kind, and amongst them we have sanity.

The road into uncertainty is the road toward psychosomatic illness, doubts, anxieties, fears, worries and vanishing awareness. As awareness is decreased, so does certainty decrease.

It is very puzzling to people at higher levels of awareness why people behave toward them as they do; such higher level people have not realized that they are not seen, much less understood. People at low levels of awareness do not observe, but substitute for observation preconceptions, evaluation and suppositions, and even physical pain by which to attain their certainties.

The mistaken use of shock by the ancient Greek upon the insane, the use of whips in old Bedlam, all sought to deliver sufficient certainty to the insane to cause them to be less insane.

Certainty delivered by blow and punishment is a non-self-determined certainty. It is productive of stimulus-response behavior. At a given stimulus a dog who has been beaten, for instance, will react invariably, providing he has been sufficiently beaten, but if he has been beaten too much, the stimulus will result only in confused bewilderment. Thus certainty delivered by blows, by applied force, eventually brings about a certainty as absolute as one could desire—total unawareness. Unconsciousness itself is a certainty which is sought by many individuals who have failed repeatedly to reach any high level of awareness certainty. These people then desire an unawareness certainty. So it seems that the thirst for certainty can lead one into oblivion if one seeks it as an effect.

An uncertainty is the product of two certainties. One of these is a conviction, whether arrived at by observation (causative) or by a blow (effected). The other is a negative certainty. One can be sure that something is and one can be sure that something is not. He can be sure that there is something, no matter what it is, present and that there is nothing present. These two certainties commingling create a condition of uncertainty known as "maybe". A "maybe" continues to be held in suspense in an individual's mind simply because he cannot decide whether it is nothing or something. He grasps and holds the certainties each time he has been given evidence or has made the decision that it is a somethingness and each time he has come to suppose that it is a nothingness. Where these two certainties of something and nothing are concerned with and can vitally influence one's continuance in a state of beingness, or where one merely supposes they can influence such a state of beingness, a condition of anxiety arises. Thus anxiety, indecision, uncertainty, a state of "maybe" can exist only in the presence of poor observation or the inability to observe.

Such a state can be remedied. One merely causes the individual to observe in terms of the three universes.

THE CONDITIONS OF EXISTENCE

There are three conditions of existence.

These three conditions comprise life.

They are BE, DO and HAVE.

The condition of BEING is defined as the assumption of a category of identity. It could be said to be the role in a game, and an example of beingness could be one's own name. Another example would be one's profession. Another example would be one's physical characteristics. Each or all of these things could be called one's *beingness*. Beingness is assumed by oneself or given to one's self or is attained, for example, in the playing of a game, each player having his own beingness.

The second condition of existence is DOING. By doing we mean action, function, accomplishment, the attainment of goals, the fulfilling of purpose, or any change of position in space.

The third condition is HAVINGNESS. By havingness, we mean owning, possessing, being capable of commanding, positioning, taking charge of objects, energies or spaces.

The essential definition of *having* is to be able to touch or permeate or to direct the disposition of.

The game of life demands that one assume a beingness in order to accomplish a doingness in the direction of havingness.

These three conditions are given in an order of seniority where life is concerned. The ability to *be* is more important than the ability to *do*. The ability to *do* is more important than the ability to *have*. In most people all three conditions are sufficiently confused that they are best understood in reverse order. When one has clarified the idea of possession or havingness, one can then proceed to clarify doingness for general activity, and when this is done one understands beingness or identity.

It is an essential to a successful existence that each of these three conditions be clarified and understood. The ability to assume or to grant beingness is probably the highest of human virtues. It is even more important to be able to permit other people to have beingness than to be able oneself to assume it.

51

MYTHS OF THE MIND

The curse of the past has been a pretense of knowledge. We've had a worship of the fable. We have had prayers being sent up to a myth. And man hasn't been looking at all.

We in this modern age of science have not developed out of the field of humanities anything comparable to a scientific observation of the mind. The humanities—psychology, sociology, criminology and the various branching studies of the social sciences in general—can be said at this time and place to have failed.

Imagining that one can see is a condition worse than being unable to see. The humanities imagined too many things to see. They never cared to look. And so they have failed.

Scientology tells you quite adequately that there is an enormous Valhalla mixed up with Pluto's realm, mixed up with fairy tales, mixed up with Menninger's work, lying all over below the level of truth. The truth is a simple thing that anybody could see. Why don't they see it? Because they live in this gorgeous wonderland which isn't and never will be.

Let's go into wonderland. The wonderland of syllables, the wonderland beneath the earth of never never. We know it as dispersal. An individual looks at something and it flashes back and he can no longer look in that direction. It kicks him in the teeth. So he mustn't look that way. He must look somewhere else. And he eventually learns very well not to observe anything.

That is the exact mechanics of how a wonderland of pretended information, which became the social sciences, was created. The individual couldn't confront man, so he turned around and developed a theory about man.

There are a lot of imaginary and legendary beings and beasts just like there were in the dark ages. Take the way the ancient mariners kept people from trading with the American Coast. Every mariner of Columbus' day believed that you just sailed so far then fell off the edge and there were terrific monsters and beasts who would drown you if you sailed beyond the sight of land.

A great many beasts had been invented to debar careless voyaging into somebody else's hunting preserves.

Now I'm not going to tell you that the field of the mind has been *only* inhabited by imaginary beings, but something of this order is done by the fellow who invents tremendous nomenclature of the brain or bone structure and then says "you have to know all these names before you can know anything about the mind" and then says "each one of these parts of the brain has a specific function." And adds "nobody should tamper with the mind because it bites."

I don't say that that is the same thing the Spanish sailor did with the sea in order to keep guys like Columbus from discovering things. I don't say that for a moment. I merely insist upon it.

All a person has to do is look—right where he is—and he will see something about the mind. But if he's been told it's very dangerous to fool with the mind and he doesn't know that those raging sea beasts are really dummies to keep fishing preserves, why, he says, "Well, I'd better not look. I'd better go blind."

Through the years I learned that they were supposed to do things with the mind across this basic premise—that I.Q. cannot change and personality characteristics are unalterable. This is a defeatism.

54

Now, Scientology is defined as knowing how to know. But it could be better defined as "summated and organized information about you". It's everything that has been known about you for 2500 years at least. But it is summated so it is communicable, so that it is applicable and so that it gets some definite results. And way over and above all these other things it is capable of changes. It can create changes for the better, and it can make things look and act better.

Most of our data is on the firm foundation of having looked. And your ability to know the subject is your ability to look.

Man, before he gets up and looks to find where he is, before he starts to look in the proper direction, discovers he's blind. Then he says, "Hey, wait a minute," and takes the veil off his eyes, takes a look—and has the tendency to keep diving into complexities.

So there is only one continuing stress in Scientology and that is greater simplicity, and that means greater communication. By involvement in a complexity we create a mystery. We sink man into a priesthood, a cult.

The simplicity of observation, the simplicity of

communication itself and only itself is functional and will take man from the bottom to the top. And the only thing I am trying to teach you is to look.

HOW TO LIVE WITH CHILDREN

An adult has certain rights around children which the children and modern adults rather tend to ignore. A good, stable adult with love and tolerance in his heart is about the best therapy a child can have.

The main consideration in raising children is the problem of training them without breaking them. You want to raise your child in such a way that you don't have to control him, so that he will be in full possession of himself at all times. Upon that depends his good behavior, his health, his sanity.

Children are not dogs. They can't be trained as dogs are trained. They are not controllable items. They are, and let's not overlook the point, men and women. A child is not a special species of animal distinct from Man. A child is a man or a woman who has not attained full growth.

Any law which applies to the behavior of men and women applies to children.

How would you like to be pulled and hauled and

ordered about and restrained from doing whatever you wanted to do? You'd resent it. The only reason a child "doesn't" resent it is because he's small. You'd half murder somebody who treated you, an adult, with the orders, contradiction and disrespect given to the average child. The child doesn't strike back because he isn't big enough. He gets your floor muddy, interrupts your nap, destroys the peace of the home instead. If he had equality with you in the matter of rights, he'd not ask this "revenge". This "revenge" is standard child behavior.

A child has a right to his self determinism. You say that if he is not restrained from pulling things down on himself, running into the road, etc., etc., he'll be hurt. What are you, as an adult, doing to make that child live in rooms or an environment where he can be hurt? The fault is yours, not his, if he breaks things.

The sweetness and love of a child is preserved only so long as he can exert his own self determinism. You interrupt that and, to a degree, you interrupt his life.

There are only two reasons why a child's right to decide for himself has to be interrupted—the fragility and danger of his environment and you, for you work out on him the things that were done to

58

you, regardless of what you think.

When you give a child something, it's his. It's not still yours. Clothes, toys, quarters, what he has been given, must remain under his exclusive control. So he tears up his shirt, wrecks his bed, breaks his fire engine. It's none of your business. How would you like to have somebody give you a Christmas present and then tell you, day after day thereafter, what you are to do with it, and even punish you if you failed to care for it the way the donor wishes? You'd wreck that donor and ruin that present. You know you would. The child wrecks your nerves when you do it to him. That's revenge. He cries. He pesters you. He breaks your things. He "accidentally" spills his milk. And he wrecks, on purpose, the possession about which he is so often cautioned. Why? Because he is fighting for his own self determinism, his own right to own and make his weight felt on his environment. This "possession" is another channel by which he can be controlled. So he has to fight the possession and the controller.

In raising your child, you must avoid "training" him into a social animal. Your child begins by being more sociable, more dignified than you are. In a relatively short time, the treatment he gets so checks him that he revolts. This revolt can be intensified until he is a terror to have around. He will be noisy,

thoughtless, careless of possessions, unclean—
anything, in short, which will annoy you. Train him,
control him and you'll lose his love. You've lost the
child forever that you seek to control and own.

Another thing is the matter of contribution. You
have no right to deny your child the right to
contribute. A human being feels able and competent
only so long as he is permitted to contribute as much
as, or more than he has contributed to him.

A baby contributes by trying to make you smile.
The baby will show off. A little later he will dance
for you, bring you sticks, try to repeat your work
motions to help you. If you do not accept those
smiles, those dances, those sticks, or those work
motions in the spirit they are given, you have begun
to interrupt the child's contribution. Now he will
start to get anxious. He will do unthinking and
strange things to your possessions in an effort to
make them "better" for you. You scold him ... that
finishes him.

Permit a child to sit on your lap. He'll sit there,
contented. Now put your arms around him and
constrain him to sit there. Do this, even though he
wasn't even trying to leave. Instantly he'll squirm.
He'll fight to get away from you. He'll get angry.
He'll cry. Recall now, he was happy before you

started to hold him. (You should actually make this experiment.)

Your efforts to mold, train, control this child in general react on him exactly like trying to hold him on your lap.

Of course, you will have difficulty if this child of yours has already been trained, controlled, ordered about, denied his own possessions. In mid-flight, you change your tactics. You try to give him his freedom. He's so suspicious of you he will have a terrible time trying to adjust. The transition period will be difficult. But, at the end of it, you'll have a well-ordered, sociable child, thoughtful of you and, very important to you, a child who loves you.

The child who is under constraint, shepherded, handled, controlled, has a very bad anxiety postulated. His parents are survival entities. They mean food, clothing, shelter, affection. This means he wants to be near them. He wants to love them, naturally, being their child.

But on the other hand, his parents are non-survival entities. His whole being and life depend upon his rights to use his own decision about his movements and his possessions and his body. Parents seek to interrupt this out of the mistaken idea that a child is

61

an idiot who won't learn unless "controlled". So he has to fight shy, to fight against, to annoy and to harrass an enemy.

Here is anxiety. "I love them dearly. I also need them. But they mean an interruption of my ability, my mind, my potential life. What am I going to do about my parents? I can't live with them. I can't live without them. Oh, dear, oh, dear!" There he sits in his rompers running this problem through his head. That problem, that anxiety, will be with him for eighteen years, more or less. And it will half wreck his life.

Freedom for the child means freedom for you.

Abandoning the possessions of the child to their fate means eventual safety for the child's possessions.

What terrible will-power is demanded of a parent not to give constant streams of directions to a child.

But it has to be done, if you want a well, a happy, a careful, a beautiful, an intelligent child!

The child has a duty toward you. He has to be able to take care of you, not an illusion that he is, but actually. And you have to have the patience to allow yourself to be cared for sloppily until, by sheer experience, itself—not by your directions—he learns how to do it well. Care for the child?—nonsense! He has probably got a better grasp of immediate situations than you have.

ON MARRIAGE

Communication is the root of marital success from which a strong union can grow, and non-communication is the rock on which the ship will bash out her keel.

In the first place, men and women aren't too careful "on whom they up and marry". In the absence of any basic training about neurosis, psychosis, or how to judge a good cook or a good wage-earner, that tricky, treacherous and not always easy-to-identify thing called "love" is the sole guiding factor in the selection of mates. It is too much to expect of a society above the level of ants to be entirely practical about an institution as basically impractical as marriage. Thus, it is not amazing that the mis-selection of partners goes on with such abandon.

There are ways, however, not only to select a marriage partner, but also to guarantee the continuation of that marriage, and these ways are simple. They depend uniformly upon communication.

There should be some parity of intellect and

sanity between a husband and wife for them to have a successful marriage. In Western culture, it is expected that the women shall have some command of the humanities and sciences. It is easy to establish the educational background of a potential marriage partner; it is not so easy to gauge their capability regarding sex, family or children, or their sanity.

In the past, efforts were made to establish sanity with ink-blots, square blocks and tests with marbles to find out if anybody had lost any. The resulting figures had to be personally interpreted with a crystal ball and then re-interpreted for application.

In Scientology, there is a test for sanity and comparative sanity which is so simple that anyone can apply it. What is the "communication lag" of the individual?—When asked a question, how long does it take him to answer? When a remark is addressed to him, how long does it take for him to register and return? The fast answer tells of the fast mind and the sane mind, providing the answer is a sequitur; the slow answer tells of down-scale. Marital partners who have the same communication lag will get along; where one partner is fast and one is slow, the situation will become unbearable to the fast partner and miserable to the slow one.

The repair of a marriage which is going on the rocks does not always require the auditing of the marriage partners. It may be that another family

65

factor is in the scene. This may be in the person of a relative, such as the mother-in-law. How does one solve this factor without using a shotgun? This, again, is simple. The mother-in-law, if there is trouble in the family, is responsible for cutting communication lines or diverting communication. One or the other of the partners, then, is cut off the communication channel on which he belongs. He senses this and objects strenuously to it.

Jealousy is the largest factor in breaking up marriages. Jealousy comes about because of the insecurity of the jealous person, and the jealousy may or may not have foundation. This person is afraid of hidden communication lines and will do anything to try to uncover them. This acts upon the other partner to make him feel that his communication lines are being cut; for he thinks himself entitled to have open communication lines, whereas his marital partner insists that he shut many of them. The resultant rows are violent, as represented by the fact that, where jealousy exists in a profession such as acting, insurance companies will not issue policies —the suicide rate is too high.

The subject of marriage could not be covered in many chapters, but here is given the basic clue to a successful marriage—Communicate!

THE MAN WHO SUCCEEDS

The conditions of success are few and easily stated.

Jobs are not held consistently and in actuality by flukes of fate or fortune. Those who depend upon luck generally experience bad luck. The ability to hold a job depends in the main upon ability. One must be able to control his work and must be able to be controlled in doing his work. One must be able, as well, to leave certain areas uncontrolled. One's intelligence is directly related to his ability. There is no such thing as being too smart. But there is such a thing as being too stupid.

But one may be both able and intelligent without succeeding. A vital part of success is the ability to handle and control, not only one's tools of the trade, but the people with whom one is surrounded. In order to do this, one must be capable of a very high level of affinity, he must be able to tolerate massive realities and he must, as well, be able to give and receive communication.

The ingredients of success are then: first, an ability to confront work with joy and not horror; a wish to do work for its own sake, not because one "has to have a paycheck". One must be able to work without driving oneself or experiencing deep depths of exhaustion. If one experiences these things, there is something wrong with him. There is some element in his environment that he should be controlling that he isn't controlling, or his accumulated injuries are such as to make him shy away from all people and masses with whom he should be in intimate contact.

The ingredients of successful work are: training and experience in the subject being addressed, good general intelligence and ability, a capability of high affinity, a tolerance of reality, and the ability to communicate and receive ideas. Given these things there is left only a slim chance of failure. Given these things a man can ignore all of the accidents of birth, marriage or fortune, for birth, marriage and fortune are not capable of placing these necessary ingredients in one's hands. One could have all the money in the world and yet be unable to perform an hour's honest labor. Such a man would be a miserably unhappy one.

The person who studiously avoids work usually works far longer and far harder than the man who pleasantly confronts it and does it. Men who cannot work are not happy men.

Work is the stable datum* of this society. Without

---

*stable datum. A datum which keeps things from being in a confusion and around which other data align.

something to do there is nothing for which to live. A man who cannot work is as good as dead and usually prefers death and works to achieve it.

The mysteries of life are not today, with Scientology, very mysterious. Mystery is not a needful ingredient. Only the very aberrated man desires to have vast secrets held away from him. Scientology has slashed through many of the complexities which have been erected for men and has bared the core of these problems. Scientology for the first time in man's history can predictably raise intelligence, increase ability, bring about a return of the ability to play a game, and permit man to escape from the dwindling spiral of his own disabilities. Therefore work itself can become a game, a pleasant and happy thing.

There is one thing which has been learned in Scientology which is very important to the state of mind of the workman. One often feels in this society that he is working for the immediate paycheck and that he does not gain for the whole society anything of any importance. He does not know several things. One of these is how few good workmen are. On the level of executives, it is interesting to note how precious any large company finds a man who can handle and control jobs and men. Such people are rare. All the empty space in the structure of this workaday world is at the top.

And there is another thing which is quite

important, and that is the fact that the world today has been led to believe, by mental philosophies calculated to betray them, that when one is dead it is all over and done with and that one has no further responsibility for anything. It is highly doubtful if this is true. One inherits tomorrow what he died out of yesterday.

Another thing we know is that men are not dispensable. It is a mechanism of old philosophies to tell men that if they think they are indispensable they should go down to the graveyard and take a look—those men were indispensable too. This is the surest foolishness. If you really looked carefully in the graveyard you would find the machinist who set the models going in yesteryear and without whom there would be no industry today. It is doubtful if such a feat is being performed just now. A workman is not just a workman. A laborer is not just a laborer. An office worker is not just an office worker. They are living, breathing, important pillars on which the entire structure of our civilization is erected. They are not cogs in a mighty machine. They are the machine itself.

ON THE DEATH OF CONSCIOUSNESS

Where does one cease to Survive and begin to Succumb? The point of demarcation is not death as we know it. It is marked by what one might call *the death of the consciousness of the individual.*

Man's greatest weapon is his reason. Lacking the teeth, the armor-plate hide, the claws of so many other life forms, Man has relied upon his ability to reason in order to further himself in his survival.

The selection of the ability to think as a chief weapon is a fortunate one. It has awarded Man with the kingdom of Earth. Reason is an excellent weapon. The animal with his teeth, with his armor-plated hide, with his long claws, is fixed with weapons he cannot alter. He cannot adjust to a changing environment. And it is terribly important to survival to change when the environment changes. Every extinct species became extinct because it could not change to control a new environment. Reason remedies this failure to a marked extent. For Man can invent new tools and new weapons and a whole new environment. Reason permits him to

71

change to fit new situations. Reason keeps him in control of new environments.

Any animal that simply adjusts itself to match its environment is doomed. Environments change rapidly. Animals that can control and change the environment have the best chance of survival.

The only way you can organize a collective state is to convince men that they must adjust and adapt themselves, like animals, to a constant environment. The people must be deprived of the right to control, as individuals, their environment. Then they can be regimented and herded into groups. They become owned, not owners. Reason and the right to reason must be taken from them, for the very center of reason is the right to make up one's own mind about one's environment.

The elements fight Man and man fights man. The primary target of the enemies of Man or a man is his right and ability to reason. The crude and blundering forces of the elements, storms, cold and night bear down against, challenge and then, mayhap, crush the Reason as well as the body.

But just as unconsciousness always precedes death, even by instants, so does the death of Reason precede the death of the organism. And this action may happen in a long span of time, even half a lifetime, even more.

Have you watched the high alertness of a young man breasting the forces which oppose life? And watched another in old age? You will find that what has suffered has been his ability to Reason. He has gained hard-won experience and on this experience he seeks, from middle age on, to travel. It is a truism that youth thinks fast on little experience. And that age thinks slowly on much. The Reason of youth is very far from always right, for youth is attempting to reason without adequate data.

Suppose we had a man who had retained all his ability to reason and yet had a great deal of experience. Suppose our gray-beards could think with all the enthusiasm and vitality of youth and yet had all their experience as well. Age says to youth, "You have no experience!" Youth says to age, "You have no vision; you will not accept or even examine new ideas!" Obviously, an ideal arrangement would be for one to have the experience of age and the vitality and vision of youth.

You may have said to yourself, "With all my experience now, what wouldn't I give for some of the enthusiasm I had once." Or perhaps, you have excused it all by saying you have "lost your illusions". But you are not sure that they were illusions. Are brightness in life, quick enthusiasm, a desire and will to live, a belief in destiny, are these things illusions? Or are they symptoms of the very stuff of which vital life is made? And isn't their decline a symptom of death?

Knowledge does not destroy a will to live. Pain and loss of self determinism destroy that will. Life can be painful. The gaining of experience is often painful. The retaining of that experience is essential. But isn't it still experience if it doesn't yet have the pain?

Suppose you could wipe out of your life all the pain, physical and otherwise, which you have accumulated. Would it be so terrible to have to part with a broken heart or a psychosomatic illness, with fears and anxieties and dreads?

Suppose a man had a chance again, with all he knows, to look life and the Universe in the eye again and say it could be whipped. Do you recall a day, when you were younger, and you woke to find bright dew sparkling on the grass, the leaves, to find the golden sun bright upon a happy world? Do you recall how beautiful and fine it once was? The first sweet kiss? The warmth of true friendship? The intimacy of a moonlight ride? What made it become otherwise than a brilliant world?

The consciousness of the world around one is not an absolute thing. One can be more conscious of color and brightness and joy at one time of life than at another. One can more easily feel the brilliant reality of things in youth than in age. And isn't this something like a decline of consciousness, of awareness?

What is it that makes us less aware of the brilliance of the world around us? Has the world changed? No, for each new generation sees the glamor and the glory, the vitality of life—the same life that age may see as dull, at best. The individual changes. And what makes him change? Is it a decay of his glands and sinews? Hardly, for all the work that has been done on glands and sinews—the structure of the body—has restored little, if any, of the brilliance of living.

"Ah, youth," sighs the adult, "if I but had your zest again!" What reduced that zest?

As one's consciousness of the brilliance of life declines, so has declined one's own consciousness. Awareness decreases exactly as consciousness decreases. The ability to perceive the world around one and the ability to draw accurate conclusions about it are, to all intents, the same thing.

75

Glasses are a symptom of the decline of consciousness. One needs one's sight bolstered to make the world look brighter. The inability to move swiftly, as one ran when one was a child, is a decline of consciousness and ability.

Complete unconsciousness is death. Half-unconsciousness is half-death. A quarter-unconsciousness is a quarter of death. And as one accumulates the pain attendant upon life and fails to accumulate the pleasures, one gradually loses one's race with the gentleman with the scythe. And there ensues, at last, the physical incapacity for seeing, for thinking and for being, as in death.

How does one accumulate this pain? And if one were to get rid of it would full consciousness and a full bright concept of life return? And is there a way to get rid of it? With Scientology, the answer is YES.

ACCENT ON ABILITY

When we say "Life", all of us know, more or less, what we are talking about; but when we use this word "Life" practically, we must examine the purposes and behavior, and in particular, the formulas evolved by Life in order to have the game called "Life".

When we say "Life", we mean Understanding; and when we say "Understanding", we mean Affinity, Reality, and Communication. To understand all would be to live at the highest level of potential action and ability. The quality of Life exists in the presence of Understanding—in the presence then, of Affinity, Reality and Communication.

Life would exist to a far less active degree in the levels of misunderstanding, incomprehensibility, psychosomatic illness, and physical and mental incapabilities. Because Life is Understanding, it attempts to understand. When it turns and faces the incomprehensible, it feels balked and baffled.

If one is obsessively, and without understanding,

being determined into incomprehensibility, then of course he is lost. Thus we discover that the only trap into which Life could fall is to do things without knowing it is doing them.

One can always understand that his ability can increase, because in the direction of an increase in ability is further understanding. Ability is dependent entirely upon a greater and better understanding of that field or area in which one cares to be more able. When one attempts to understand inability he is of course looking at less comprehensibility, less understanding, and so does not then understand lessening ability anywhere near as well as he understands increasing ability. In the absence of understanding of ability we get a fear of loss of ability, which is simply the fear of an unknown or a thought-to-be-unknowable thing, for there is less knownness and less understanding in less ability.

Part of understanding and ability is control. Of course, it is not necessary to control everything everywhere if one totally understands them. However, in a lesser understanding of things, and of course in the spirit of having a game, control becomes a necessary factor. The anatomy of control is Start, Stop and Change, and this is fully as important to know as Understanding itself, and as the triangle which composes Understanding:

78

Affinity, Reality and Communication.

The doctors and nurses in a contagious ward have some degree of control over the illnesses which they see before them. It is only when they begin to recognize their inability to handle these ills or these patients that they, themselves, succumb to these. In view of the fact that of recent centuries we have been very successful in handling contagious diseases, doctors and nurses, then, can walk with impunity through contagious wards.

The fighters of disease, having some measure of control over the disease, are then no longer afraid of the disease and so it cannot affect them. Of course, there would be a level of body understanding on this which might yet still mirror fear, but we would have the same statement obtaining. People who are able to control something do not need to be afraid of it and do not suffer ill effects from it. People who cannot control things can receive bad effects from those things.

The common denominator of all neurosis, psychosis, aberration and psychosomatic ills is "can't work". Any nation which has a high incidence of these is reduced in production and is reduced in longevity.

79

Amongst the unable is the criminal, who is *unable* to think of the other fellow, *unable* to determine his own actions, *unable* to follow orders, *unable* to make things grow, unable to determine the difference between good and evil, unable to think at all on the future. Anybody has some of these; the criminal has *all* of them.

And what does one do about "how bad it is"? Well, if one depends for a long time upon others to do something about it, or depends upon force, he will fail. From his viewpoint the only one who can put more Life, more Understanding, more Tolerance and more Capability into the environment is himself. Just by existing in a state of higher Understanding, just by being more capable, an individual could resolve for those around him many of their problems and difficulties.

The accent is on ability.

HONEST PEOPLE HAVE RIGHTS, TOO

After you have achieved a high level of ability, you will be the first to insist upon your rights to live with honest people.

When you know the technology of the mind, you know that it is a mistake to use "individual rights" and "freedom" as arguments to protect those who would only destroy.

Individual rights were not originated to protect criminals, but to bring freedom to honest men. Into this area of protection then dived those who needed "freedom" and "individual liberty" to cover their own questionable activities.

Freedom is for honest people. No man who is not himself honest can be free—he is in his own trap. When his own deeds cannot be disclosed, then he is a prisoner; he must withhold himself from his fellows and is a slave to his own conscience. Freedom must be deserved before any freedom is possible.

To protect dishonest people is to condemn them

81

to their own hells. By making "individual rights" a synonym for "protect the criminal" one helps bring about a slave state for all, for where "individual liberty" is abused, an impatience with it arises which at length sweeps us all away. The targets of all disciplinary laws are the few who err. Such laws, unfortunately, also injure and restrict those who do not err. If all were honest, there would be no disciplinary threats.

There is only one way out for a dishonest person—facing up to his own responsibilities in the society and putting himself back into communication with his fellow man, his family, the world at large. By seeking to invoke his "individual rights" to protect himself from an examination of his deeds, he reduces, just that much, the future of individual liberty—for he himself is not free. Yet he infects others who are honest by using *their* right to freedom to protect himself.

Uneasy lies the head that wears a guilty conscience.

And it will lie no more easily by seeking to protect misdeeds by pleas of "freedom means that you must never look at me". The right of a person to survive is directly related to his honesty.

82

Freedom for man does not mean freedom to injure man. Freedom of speech does not mean freedom to harm by lies.

Man cannot be free while there are those amongst him who are slaves to their own terrors.

The mission of a techno-space society is to subordinate the individual and control him by economic and political duress. The only casualty in a machine age is the individual and his freedom.

To preserve that freedom one must not permit men to hide their evil intentions under the protection of that freedom. To be free, a man must be honest with himself and with his fellows.

If a man uses his own honesty to protest the unmasking of dishonesty, then that man is an enemy of his own freedom.

We can stand in the sun only so long as we don't let the deeds of others bring the darkness.

Freedom is for the honest men. Individual liberty exists only for those who have the ability to be free.

Who would punish when he could salvage?

Only a madman would break a wanted object he could repair.

The individual must not die in this machine age—rights or no rights. The criminal and madman must not triumph with their new-found tools of destruction.

The least free person is the person who cannot reveal his own acts and who protests the revelation of the improper acts of others. On such people will be built a future political slavery where we all have numbers—and our guilt—unless we act.

It is fascinating that blackmail and punishment are the keynotes of all dark operations. What would happen if these two commodities no longer existed? What would happen if all men were free enough to speak? Then and only then, would you have freedom.

On the day when we can fully trust each other, there will be peace on Earth.

ACCEPTANCE LEVEL

One thing that a person will discover is that he has been carefully taught that certain things are bad and, therefore, not enjoyable and that he has set up resistances to these things and that they, at length— these resistances—have become a sponge for the things they were set up to counteract and the resistance, caving in, has created a hunger for that which was, at first, resisted.

This is the physical universe at work in its very best operation: Make one fight something, then so arrange it that one winds up craving for what one was fighting.

You can, if you look about you, see Acceptance Level dramatized in every activity of life. You can understand, then, why some woman will not clean up a living room; a living room is not acceptable, except in a cluttered fashion to this person. You can understand, also, why some man leaves a beautiful and helpful girl and runs off with a maid or a prostitute; his acceptance level was too far below the beautiful girl. You can understand, too, some of you, why you were not acceptable in your own homes when you were young; you were too bright and too cheerful and this was too high above those around you. You can understand, as well, why the newspapers print the stories they do.

CONFRONTING

That which a person can confront, he can handle.

The first step of handling anything is gaining an ability to face it.

It could be said that war continues as a threat to man because man cannot confront war. The idea of making war so terrible that no one will be able to fight it is the exact reverse of fact—if one wishes to end war. The invention of the long bow, gun powder, heavy naval cannon, machine guns, liquid fire, and the hydrogen bomb add only more and more certainty that war *will* continue. As each new element which man cannot confront is added to elements he has not been able to confront so far, man engages himself upon a decreasing ability to handle war.

We are looking here at the basic anatomy of all problems. Problems start with an inability to confront anything. Whether we apply this to domestic quarrels or to insects, to garbage dumps or Picasso, one can always trace the beginning of any existing problem to an unwillingness to confront.

Let us take a domestic scene. The husband or the wife cannot confront the other, cannot confront second dynamic* consequences, cannot confront the economic burdens, and so we have domestic strife. The less any of these actually are confronted, the more problem they will become.

It is a truism that one never solves anything by running away from it. Of course, one might also say that one never solves cannon balls by baring his breast to them. But I assure you that if nobody cared whether cannon balls were fired or not, control of people by threat of cannon balls would cease.

Down on Skid Row where flotsam and jetsam exist to keep the police busy, we could not find one man whose basic difficulties, whose downfall could not be traced at once to an inability to confront. A criminal once came to me whose entire right side was paralyzed. Yet, this man made his living by walking up to people in alleys, striking them and robbing

*second dynamic. Urge to survive through sex and children. The dynamics are urges to survive as and through self (first dynamic), sex and children (second dynamic), groups (third dynamic), mankind (fourth dynamic), all life forms (fifth dynamic), the physical universe—matter, energy, space and time (sixth dynamic), spirits or thought (seventh dynamic), and The Supreme Being, The Creator, Infinity (eighth dynamic).

them. Why he struck people he could not connect with his paralyzed side and arm. From his infancy he had been educated not to confront men. The nearest he could come to confronting men was to strike them, and so his criminal career.

The more the horribleness of crime is deified by television and public press, the less the society will be able to handle crime. The more formidable is made the juvenile delinquent, the less the society will be able to handle the juvenile delinquent.

In education, the more esoteric and difficult a subject is made, the less the student will be able to handle the subject. When a subject is made too formidable by an instructor, the more the student retreats from it. There were, for instance, some early European mental studies which were so complicated and so incomprehensible and which were sewn with such lack of understanding of man that no student could possibly confront them.

Man, at large today, is in this state with regard to the human spirit. For centuries man was educated to believe in demons, ghouls, and things that went boomp in the night. There was an organization in southern Europe which capitalized upon this terror and made demons and devils so formidable that at length man could not even face the fact that any of

89

his fellows had souls. And thus we entered an entirely materialistic age. With the background teaching that no one can confront the "invisible", vengeful religions sought to move forward into a foremost place of control. Naturally, it failed to achieve its goal and irreligion became the order of the day, thus opening the door for Communism and other idiocies. Although it might seem true that one cannot confront the invisible, who said that a spirit was *always* invisible? Rather, let's say that it is impossible for man or anything else to confront the nonexistent; and thus when nonexistent gods are invented and are given more roles in the society, we discover man becomes so degraded that he cannot even confront the spirit in his fellows, much less become moral.

Confronting, as a subject in itself, is intensely interesting. Indeed, there is some evidence that mental image pictures occur only when the individual is unable to confront the circumstances of the picture. When this compounds and man is unable to confront anything anywhere, he might be considered to have pictures of everything, everywhere. This is proven by a rather interesting test made in 1947 by myself. I discovered, although I did not entirely interpret it at the time, that an individual has no further pictures when he can confront all pictures; thus being able to confront everything he has done, he is no longer troubled with the things he has done. Supporting this, it will be discovered that individuals who progress in an ability to handle pictures eventually have no pictures at all. This we call a "Clear".

A "Clear", in an absolute sense, would be someone who could confront anything and everything in the past, present and future.

The handling of a problem seems to be simply the increase of ability to confront the problem, and when the problem can be totally confronted, it no longer exists. This is strange and miraculous.

Man's difficulties are a compound of his cowardices. To have difficulties in life, all it is necessary to do is to start running away from the business of livingness. After that, problems of unsolvable magnitude are assured. When individuals are restrained from confronting life, they accrue a vast ability to have difficulties with it.

Various nervous traits can be traced at once by *trying to* confront with something which insists on running away. A nervous hand, for instance, would be a hand with which the individual is trying to confront something. The forward motion of the nervousness would be the effort to make it confront;

the backward motion of it would be its refusal to confront. Of course, the basic error is confronting *with* the hand.

The world is never bright to those who cannot confront it. Everything is a dull gray to a defeated army. The whole trick of somebody telling you "it's all bad over there" is contained in the fact that he is trying to keep you from confronting something and thus make you retreat from life. Eye glasses, nervous twitches, tensions, all of these things stem from an unwillingness to confront. When that willingness is repaired, these disabilities tend to disappear.

ON BRINGING ORDER

When you start to introduce order into anything, disorder shows up and blows off. Therefore, efforts to bring order in the society or any part of it will be productive of disorder for a while every time.

The trick is to keep on bringing order; and soon the disorder is gone, and you have orderly activity remaining. But if you *hate* disorder and fight disorder only, don't ever try to bring order to anything, for the resulting disorder will drive you half mad.

Only if you can ignore disorder and can understand this principle, can you have a working world.

ON HUMAN CHARACTER

In the past, a knowledge of his own character was an unpalatable fact to Man, since people sought to force him to achieve that knowledge solely through condemnation. He resisted what he was, and he became what he resisted; and ever with a dwindling spiral, he reached lower dregs. If ever once a man were to realize with accuracy what he was, if he were to realize what other people sought to make him, if he could attain this knowledge with great certainty, there are no chains strong enough to prevent his escaping; for such would be his astonishment that he would brave beasts, gods and Lucifer himself to become something better than what he had beheld in his own heart.

The only tragedy of all this is that Man has lacked any method of estimating himself with certainty so as to know what it was he was trying to improve.

The basic impulse of Man is to produce an effect.

In relatively high-toned beings, the very upper range of Man and above, the impulse is to produce something out of nothing. One can only cause a creative effect by causing nothingnesses to become something.

Lower on the tone scale*, the effect most desired is to make nothing out of something. The general range of Man occupies this area of the scale.

Man on the lower ranges is entirely dedicated to the goals of the body itself. The body, to exist, must make nothing out of something. This, as the simplest illustration, is the goal of eating. It may or may not be necessary to life to eat; it may not even be necessary for the body to eat. In Para-Scientology**, there is some evidence that the stomach once produced sufficient life energy to motivate the body without any further "food", but the body of man and beasts in general is not equipped so today, and of that we are very certain.

The body's single effort to make something out of nothing is resident in sex, and in this culture at our time, sex is a degraded and nasty thing which must

---

*tone scale. The scale of emotional states which range from death at the bottom, up through apathy, grief, fear, covert hostility, anger, antagonism, boredom, cheerfulness, conservatism to enthusiasm at the top (actually higher and lower tone levels exist than those named).
**Para-Scientology. Any part of Scientology that exceeds the reality of an individual at any given time.

be hidden at best and babies are something not to have, but to be prevented. Thus, even sex has been made to parallel the something-into-nothing impulse.

Exactly as the body, by eating, seeks to make nothing out of something, so does the general run of Man, in his conversation and inter-personal relationship, seek to make a nothingness out of friendship, acquaintances, himself, art and all other things. He much more readily accepts a statement or a news story which reduces something further toward nothing than he accepts a story which raises from a relative nothing to a higher something. Thus, we find out that scientific achievements for the good of man occupy a very late place in the newspapers and stories of murders and love-nests, wars and plagues, gain first place.

Man, in his present form, is held on the road to survival by his culture alone. This culture has been policed into action by brute force. The bulk of men are surviving against their own will. They are working against their own desires, and they seek, wherever possible and ever so covertly, to succumb.

The physical universe could be called a Love-Hate universe, for these two are the most prominently displayed features, and neither one has any great altitude, although many claim that love is all and that love is high on the tone scale, which it is not.

To live, Man must eat. Every time a man eats, no matter the kindness of his heart or disposition, something must have died or must die, even though it is only cells. To eat, then, one must be able to bring about death. If eating is motivated by death, then digestion would be as good as one is permitted to kill. Digestions are bad in this society. Killing is shunned in a degraded and covert fashion, and man eats only those things which not only have been killed elsewhere and out of his sight, but have as well been certified as dead through scalding cookery. Killing even food is today far above the ability of the majority of our culture.

The characteristics of love could be said to be No-Kill, stomach trouble, hunger but can't eat, work, flows, heavy emphasis on affinity, reality and communication, and inhibited sex. Hate as a personality could be said to characterize, at least on a thought level, kill, bowel trouble, hungry but eats covertly, no work, hold, pretended affinity, reality and communication, and enforced sex. These are two personality classes. Many people are compounded of both.

Thought in Man is largely born out of impact and

97

is not free. It is an effort to know before he knows, which is to say, to prevent a future. The phenomenon of going into the past is simply the phenomenon of trying to take the knowledge which one acquired through force and impact and held after the event, and place it before the event so as to prevent that thing which has already happened. "If I had only known" is a common phrase. This gets bad enough to cause man to want to know before he looks at anything, for in his debased state it is dangerous not only to use force, not only to use emotion, not only to think, but also to perceive things which do. Thus the prevalence of glasses in this society.

The body—and that means, of course, Man in this culture—must have a reason for everything. That which has the most reason is the body. A reason is an explanation, the way Man interprets it, and he feels he has to explain himself away and to explain every action which he makes. Man believes he must have force but receives force, that he must not perceive or be perceived, that he must kill but must not be killed, that he must not have emotion, that he must be able to wreak destruction without receiving it. He can have no pain; he must shun work and pretend that all work he does has a definite goal. Everything he sees he feels must have been created by something else and he himself must not create. Everything has a prior creation to his own. All things

98

must be based on earlier things. Thus, he shuns responsibility for whatever he makes and whatever destruction he may create.

This animal has equipped himself with weapons of destruction far superior to his weapons for healing and in this low-toned mockery whines and pleads that he is duplicating saintliness and godliness, yet he knows no meaning of ethics and can follow only morals. He is a meat animal, a thing in the straitjacket of a police force, made to survive, made to stay in check, made to do his duty and performing most of it without joy and without, poor thing, even actual suffering. He is a meat animal; he is something to be eaten. If he is to be helped, he must learn where he is and find better.

In our current age, cowardice is an accepted social pose; self-abnegation, a proper mode of address; hidden indecency, a proper method of survival.

It may be that my statement of this does not carry through with an entire conviction. Fortunately, although these data are based on a wide experience with Man, particularly in the last few years, as well as during a terrible and cataclysmic war, my statement of the case does not have to stand, for in Scientology we have the processes which signify the accuracy of this observation on human character.

PAST, PRESENT AND FUTURE

There is a basic rule that a psychotic person is concerned with the past, a neurotic person is barely able to keep up with the present, and a sane person is concerned with the future.

This division could be more specifically made by realizing that the neurotic is barely able to confront the present, but that the very, very sane confront the present entirely and have very little concern for the future, being competent enough in handling the present to let the future take care of itself. Looking into the past and looking into the extreme future, alike, are efforts to avoid present time and efforts to look elsewhere than *at* something.

You have known people who would reply on an entirely different subject when asked about anything; when consulted concerning the weather, they would reply about a meteorologist. The inability to look *at* something becomes first manifest by thinking before looking, and then the actual target at which one should be looking is more and more avoided until it is hidden entirely in a mixup of complications.

100

The avoidance of reality is merely an avoidance of present time.

An individual who will not look at the physical universe must look either ahead of it into the future, or behind it into the past. One of the reasons he does this is because there is insufficient action in the present to begin with; and then this thirst for action develops into an inability to have action, and he decides that all must be maintained in a constant state, and he seeks to prevent action. This also applies to pain. People who are somewhat out of present time have a horrible dread of pain; and people who are truly out of present time—as in a psychotic state—have a revulsion towards pain which could not be described. A person entirely within present time is not much concerned with pain.

The avoidance of work is one of the best indicators of a decayed state on the part of a personality. There are two common denominators to all aberrated personalities; one of these is a horror of work and the other is a horror of pain. People only mildly out of present time, which is to say people who are categorized as "sane", have already started to apologize about work, in that they work toward an end reward and no longer consider that the output of effort itself and the accomplishment of things is sufficient reward in itself. Thus, the whole network of gratitude or admiration becomes necessary pay for energy put forth. The parental

101

demand for gratitude is often reflected in a severely aberrated person who is given to feel he can never repay the enormous favors conferred on him by being worked for by his parents. Actually, they need not to be paid, for, flatly, if it was not sufficient reward to do the work of raising him, they are beyond being paid; in other words, they could not accept pay.

Taking the very, very sane person in present time, one would mark a decline of his sanity by a shift from an interest in present time to an overwhelming interest in the future which would decline into considerable planning for the future in order to avoid bad things happening in it, to, then, a shunning of the future because of painful incidents, to a shuddering and tenuous hold on present time, and, finally, to an avoidance of both the future and present time and a shift into the past. This last would be a psychotic state.

One holds on to things in the past on the postulate that they must not happen in the future. This sticks the person in the past.

Inaction and indecision in the present is because of fear of consequences of the future. In Scientology this condition in an individual can be remedied so that he can more comfortably face present time.

102

PLAYING THE GAME

The highest activity is playing a game. When one is high-toned, he knows that it is a game. As he falls away down the tone scale, he becomes less and less aware of the game.

The greatest ability of thought is DIFFERENTIATION. So long as one can differentiate, one is sane. Its opposite is IDENTIFICATION.

The legal definition of sanity is the "ability to tell right from wrong".

Therefore, the highest ability in playing a game would be the ability to know the rightness and wrongness rules of that particular game. As all rightness and wrongness are considerations and as the game itself is a consideration, the playing of the game requires a high ability to differentiate, particularly it requires an ability to know the rules and the right-rules and the wrong-rules.

When an individual is prone to identify, he is no longer able to differentiate the right-rules and the wrong-rules, and the right-rules become wrong and the wrong-rules become right, and we have a criminal.

A criminal cannot play the game of society. He plays, then, the "game" called "cops and robbers".

A person who strongly identifies is not necessarily a criminal, but he certainly is having trouble playing the game of society. Instead of playing that game, he "gets tired", "gets sick". He has these things happen because he doesn't want to play the social game. He has a "game" of sorts in "hypochondria".

Now, if you had a culture which was running a no-game game for anybody, a culture which itself had no game for everybody to play, a culture which had in its government a fixation on keeping anyone from playing the game THEY wanted to play, we would have, as its manifestation, all manner of curious ills, such as those described in various ideologies like Capitalism or Communism. The entire government game would be "Stop playing YOUR game". The degree of sanity in government would be the degree it permitted strong and active participation in the game of government, in the game of playing your game.

But if people who can't play the game can't

differentiate, similarly, a sane person could find himself very confused to be part of a game which wasn't differentiating and where the rightness and wrongness rules were unclearly defined. Thus, a government without exact and accurate codes and jurisprudence would discover in its citizens an inability to play the game no matter how sane they were.

Thus, the game can be crazy and its players sane, or the players can be crazy and the game sane. Either condition would affect the other. When we get crazy players and a crazy game, the end product of either of the two imbalances above, we would get anything except a game. We would get chaos.

As a useful example of an inability to differentiate, let us take people who cannot see anything wrong with slanderous materials. We have here people who see no difference. They don't differentiate. They don't differentiate, because they see no game. They see no game because they can't play a game. Or, habituated to a social structure which had no rules of rightness or wrongness, they have lost their criteria.

FREEDOM *vs.* ENTRAPMENT

In Greece, Rome, England, Colonial America, France and Washington, a great deal of conversation is made on the subject of Freedom. Freedom, apparently, is something that is very desirable. Indeed, Freedom is seen to be the goal of a nation or a people. Similarly, if we are restoring ability to a person, we must restore Freedom. If we do not restore Freedom, we cannot restore ability. The muscle-bound wrestler, the tense driver, the rocket jockey with frozen reaction time alike are not able. Their ability lies in an increase of Freedom, a release of tension, and a better communication to their environment.

The main trouble with Freedom is that it does not have an anatomy. Something that is free is free. It is not free with wires, vias, by-passes, or dams; it is simply free. There is something else about Freedom which is intensely interesting—it cannot be erased.

You may be able to concentrate somebody's attention on something that is not free and thus bring him into a state of belief that Freedom does not exist, but this does not mean that you have erased the individual's freedom. You have not. All the freedom he ever had is still there.

Furthermore, Freedom has no quantity, and by definition, it has no location in space or time. Thus we see the individual (spirit, soul) as potentially the freest thing there could be. Thus man concentrates upon Freedom.

But if Freedom has no anatomy, then please explain how one is going to attain to something which cannot be fully explained. If anyone talks about a "road to Freedom", he is talking about a linear line. This, then, must have boundaries. If there are boundaries, there is no Freedom.

Talk to a person who works from eight o'clock until five with no goals, and no future, and no belief in the organization and its goals, who is being required by time-payments, rent, and other barriers of an economic variety to invest all of his salary as soon as it is paid, and we have an individual who has lost the notion of Freedom. His concentration is so thoroughly fixed upon barriers that Freedom has to be in terms of less barriers.

Life is prone to a stupidity in many cases in which it is not cognizant of a disaster until the disaster has

107

occurred. The mid-western farmer had a phrase for it: "Lock the door after the horse is stolen." It takes a disaster in order to educate people into the existence of such a disaster. This is education by pain, by impact, by punishment. Therefore, a population which is faced with a one-shot disaster which will obliterate the sphere would not have a chance to learn very much about the sphere before it was obliterated. Thus, if they insisted upon learning by experience in order to prevent such a disaster, they would never have the opportunity. If no atomic bomb of any kind had been dropped in World War II, it is probable there would be no slightest concern about atomic fission, although atomic fission might have been developed right on up to the planet-buster without ever being used against Man, and then the planet-buster being used on Earth, and so destroying it.

If a person did not know what a tiger was, and we desired to demonstrate to him that no tigers were present, we would have a difficult time of it. Here we have a freedom from tigers without knowing anything about tigers. Before he could understand an absence of tigers, he would have to understand the presence of tigers. This is the process of learning we know as "by experience".

In order to know anything, if we are going to use

educational methods, it is necessary then, to know, as well, its opposite. The opposite of tigers probably exists in Malayan jungles where tigers are so frequent that the absence of tigers would be a novelty, indeed. A country which was totally burdened by tigers might not understand at all the idea that there were no tigers. In some parts of the world, a great deal of argument would have to be entered into with the populace of a tiger-burdened area to get them to get any inkling of what an absence of tigers would be.

The understanding of Freedom, then, is slightly complex if, then, individuals who do not have it are not likely to understand it.

But the opposite of Freedom is slavery and everybody knows this—or is it? I do not think these two things are a dichotomy. Freedom is not the plus of a condition where slavery is the minus, unless we are dealing entirely with the political organism. Where we are dealing with the individual, better terminology is necessary and more understanding of the anatomy of minus-Freedom is required.

Minus-Freedom is entrapment. Freedom is the absence of barriers. Less Freedom is the presence of barriers. Entirely minus-Freedom would be the omnipresence of barriers. A barrier is matter or energy or time or space. The more matter, energy, time or space assumes command over the individual, the less Freedom that individual has. This is best understood as entrapment, since slavery connotes an intention and entrapment might be considered almost without intention. A person who falls into a bear-pit might not have intended to fall into it at all, and a bear-pit might not have intended a person to fall upon its stake. Nevertheless, an entrapment has occurred. The person is in the bear-pit.

If one wants to understand existence and his unhappiness with it, he must understand entrapment and its mechanisms.

In what can a person become entrapped? Basically and foremost, he can become entrapped in ideas. In view of the fact that freedom and ability can be seen to be somewhat synonymous, then ideas of disability are, first and foremost, an entrapment. I daresay that, amongst men, the incident has occurred that a person has been sitting upon a bare plain in the total belief that he is entirely entrapped by a fence.

There is that incident mentioned in *Self-Analysis** of fishing in Lake Tanganyika where the sun's rays,

*Self Analysis by L. Ron Hubbard available from your local bookstores and the bookstores of Hubbard Scientology Organizations, listed in back pages.

being equatorial, pierce burningly to the lake's bottom. The natives there fish by tying a number of slats of wood on a long piece of line. They take either end of this line and put it in canoes, and then paddle the two canoes to shore, the slatted line stretching between. The sun shining downward presses the shadows of these bars down to the bottom of the lake, and thus a cage of shadows moves inward toward the shallows. The fish, seeing this cage contract upon them, which is composed of nothing but the absence of light, flounder frantically into the shallows where they cannot swim and are thus caught, picked up in baskets and cooked. There is nothing to be afraid of but shadows.

When we move out of mechanics, man finds himself on unsure ground. The idea that ideas could be so strong and pervasive is foreign to most men.

So, first and foremost, we have the idea. Then, themselves the product of ideas, we have the more obvious mechanics of entrapment in matter, energy, space and time.

The anatomy of entrapment is an interesting one, and the reason why people get entrapped, and indeed, the total mechanics of entrapment, are now understood. In Scientology a great deal of experimentation was undertaken to determine the factors

111

which resulted in entrapment, and it was discovered that the answer to the entire problem was two-way communication.

Roughly, the laws back of this are: Fixation occurs in the presence of one-way communication. Entrapment occurs only when one has not given or received answers to the things entrapping him.

It could be said that all the entrapment there is is the waiting one does for an answer.

Entrapment is the opposite of Freedom. A person who is not free is trapped. He may be trapped by an idea, he may be trapped by matter, he may be trapped by energy, he may be trapped by space, he may be trapped by time, he may be trapped by all of them. The more thoroughly a person is trapped the less free he is. He cannot change, he cannot move, he cannot communicate, he cannot feel affinity and reality. Death itself could be said to be Man's ultimate in entrapment, for when a man is totally entrapped he is dead.

The component parts of Freedom, as we first gaze upon it, are then: Affinity, Reality and Communication, which summate into Understanding. Once Understanding is attained, Freedom is obtained. For the individual who is thoroughly snarled in the mechanics of entrapment, it is necessary to restore to him sufficient communication to permit his ascendence into a higher state of understanding. Once this has been accomplished his entrapment is ended.

A greater freedom can be attained by the individual. The individual does desire a greater freedom, once he has some inkling of it. And Scientology steers the individual out of the first areas of entrapment to a point where he can gain higher levels of Freedom.

JUSTICE

What *is* justice?

"The quality of mercy is not strained—it droppeth as the gentle rain from heaven . . ." may be poetic, but it is not definitive. It does, however, demonstrate that even in Shakespeare's time men were adrift on the subject of justice, injustice, severity and mercy.

People speak of an action as unjust or an action as just. What do they mean? Yet, unless we can understand exactly what is meant by these terms, we certainly cannot undertake to evaluate the actions of individuals, communities and nations. For the lack of an ability to so evaluate, misunderstandings come about which have, in the past, led to combative personal relationships and, on the international scene, to war. An individual or a nation fails or refuses to understand the measures taken by another or fails to fall within the agreement of the pattern to which others are accustomed and chaos results.

In Scientology the following definitions now

exist:

JUSTICE—The impartial administration of the laws of the land in accordance with the extant level of the severity-mercy ratio of the people.

LAWS—The codified agreements of the people crystallizing their customs and representing their believed-in necessities of conduct.

MERCY—A lessening away from the public's acceptance of discipline necessary to guarantee their mutual security.

SEVERITY—An increase in that discipline believed necessary by the people to guarantee their security.

INJUSTICE—Failure to administer existing law.

EQUITY—Any civil procedure holding citizens responsible to citizens which delivers decision to persons in accordance with the general expectancy in such cases.

RIGHTS—The franchises of citizenship according to existing codes.

When laws are not derived from custom or when a

new law contravenes an uncancelled old law, exact law becomes confused and injustice is then inevitable.

Basic justice can occur only when codified law or a majority-held custom exists.

Observing these definitions, jurisprudence only then becomes possible. Law Courts, legislatures and legislation become confused, as nothing is possible in the absence of an understanding of such principles.

Laws which do not derive from agreement amongst the society which we call custom, are unenforceable unless there is then a widespread agreement that this is customary in the society. No matter how many police are hired, no matter the purity of prose with which the legislation is written, no matter the signatures occurring on the enforcing document, the public will not obey that law. Similarly, when a government acts to ignore certain basic customs amongst the people and refuses to enforce them, that government then finds itself in a state of civil turmoil with its people on that subject. We can look at any public-government battle and discover that it stems exactly from a violation of these principles.

An understanding on the part of a nation of the

116

difficulties of another is necessary to a continued peace. When one nation begins to misunderstand the motives and justices conceived necessary by another nation, stress sets up which eventually leads to war, all too often.

Whenever there is an excessive commotion amongst a people against its government, the government is then invited to act as an opponent to the people. If a government is acting toward its people as though it were an opponent of the people and not a member of the team, it becomes obvious that many of these points must exist in the law codes of the country and must violate the customs of the people. Wherever such a point exists, turbulence results.

*   *   *

And that is justice.

THE VOCABULARIES OF SCIENCE

In all scientific systems you have a number of code words which operate as communication carriers, and when a person does not know these words well, he is having difficulty with the science itself. I have seen a senior in science falling down in his comprehension of a later part of the science because he had never gotten the nomenclature of the science straight to begin with. He did not know exactly what a British Thermal Unit was, or something like that—therefore, later on, when he's solving some vast and involved problem, there's a datum rambling around in his head and it's not stable at all—it's getting confused —it's mixed up with all other data. And that is only because he didn't understand what the *term* was in the first place.

So just as you learn semaphore signals, just as you learn Morse Code, just as you learn baby talk, so, when you become conversant with any particular specialized subject, you must become conversant with its terminology. Your understanding of it then increases. Otherwise, understanding is impeded by these words rattling around and not joining themselves to anything. If you know vaguely that such and such a word exists and yet have no definite understanding of what it means, it does not align. Thus, a misunderstanding of a word can cause a misalignment of a subject, and this really is the basis of the primary confusion in Man's understanding of the mind.

There have been so many words assigned to various parts of the mind that one would be staggered if he merely catalogued all of these things. Take, for instance, the tremendous background and technology of psychoanalysis. Overpoweringly complicated material, most of it is merely descriptive; some of it, action terminology, such as the censor, the id, the ego, the alter-ego, and what not. Most of these things lined up, each one meaning a specific thing. But the practitioners who began to study this science did not have a good founding in the exact sciences—in other words, they didn't have a model of the exact sciences. And in the humanities, they could be as careless as they liked with their words, because the humanities were not expected to be precise or exact—not a criticism of them—it just means that you could have a lesser command of the language.

When they got into the study of Freud, they got into this interesting thing—to one person an id was

119

one thing and to another person it was something else. And alter-ego was this and it was that. The confusion of terms there, practically all by itself, became the totality of confusion of psychoanalysis.

Actually, psychoanalysis is as easy to understand, certainly, as Japanese. Japanese is a baby talk—very, very hard to read, very, very easy to talk. If you can imagine a language which tells you which is the subject, which is the verb, which is the object, every time it speaks, you can imagine this baby-talk kind of a language. One that doesn't have various classes or conjugations of verbs. A very faint kind of a language. Nevertheless, it merely consists, in order to communicate with a Japanese, of knowing the meanings of certain words; and if you know the meanings of those words precisely, then when a Japanese comes up to you and says, "Do you want a cup of tea?", you don't immediately get up because you thought he said, "Wet Paint". You have a communication possibility.

Well, similarly, with the language of psycho-analysis, the great difficulties inherent in under-standing such a thing as psychoanalysis became much less difficult when one viewed psychoanalysis as a code system to relay certain meanings. It did not, then, become a problem of whether or not these phenomena existed or didn't exist. It simply became a problem of words meaning a certain precise thing. And if they meant that thing to everybody, then everybody was talking psychoanalysis, and if it didn't mean this thing to everybody, then people weren't talking psychoanalysis. Who knows *what* they were talking? The next thing you know, they were talking Jungianism—the next thing you know, they were talking Adlerianism—and the amount of difference between these various items is minute, to say the least. But the language difficulties, then, made many practitioners in that field at odds with the theory, which they did not, at any rate, understand.

I remember one time learning Igoroti, an Eastern primitive language, in a single night. I sat up by kerosene lantern and took a list of words that had been made by an old missionary in the hills in Luzon—the Igorot had a very simple language. This missionary had phoneticized their language and he had made a list of their main words and their usage and grammar. And I remember sitting up under a mosquito net with the mosquitoes hungrily chomping their beaks just outside the net, and learning this language—three hundred words—just memorizing these words and what they meant. And the next day I started to get them in line and align them with people, and was speaking Igoroti in a very short time.

The point here is that it is not difficult to learn a language, if you understand that you are learning a language.

HOW TO STUDY A SCIENCE

The whole subject of a science, as far as the student is concerned, is good or bad in direct ratio to his knowledge of it. It is up to a student to find out how precise the tools are. He should, before he starts to discuss, criticize or attempt to improve on the data presented to him, find out for himself whether or not the mechanics of a science are as stated and whether or not it does what has been proposed for it.

He should make up his mind about each thing that is taught in the school. The procedure, techniques, mechanics and theory. He should ask himself these questions: Does this piece of data exist? Is it true? Does it work? Will it produce the best possible results in the shortest time?

There are two ways man ordinarily accepts things, neither of them very good. One is to accept a statement because Authority says it is true and must be accepted, and the other is by preponderance of agreement amongst other people.

Preponderance of agreement is all too often the

general public test for sanity or insanity. Suppose someone were to walk into a crowded room and suddenly point to a ceiling saying, "Oh, look! There's a huge, twelve-foot spider on the ceiling!" Everyone would look up, but no one else would see the spider. Finally someone would tell him so. "Oh, yes, there is" he would declare, and become very angry when he found that no one would agree with him. If he continued to declare his belief in the existence of the spider, he would very soon find himself institutionalized.

The basic definition of sanity, in this somewhat nebulously learned society, is whether or not a person agrees with everyone else. It is a very sloppy manner of accepting evidence, but all too often it is the primary measuring stick.

And then the Rule of Authority: "Does Dr. J. Doe agree with your proposition? No? Then, of course, it cannot be true. Dr. Doe is an eminent authority in the field."

A man by the name of Galen at one time dominated the field of medicine. Another man by the name of Harvey upset Galen's cozy position with a new theory of blood circulation. Galen had been agreeing with the people of his day concerning the "tides" of the blood. They knew nothing about heart action. They accepted everything they had been taught and did little observing of their own. Harvey worked at the Royal Medical Academy and found by animal vivisection the actual function of the heart.

He had the good sense to keep his findings absolutely quiet for a while. Leonardo da Vinci had somehow discovered or postulated the same thing, but he was a "crazy artist" and no one would believe an artist. Harvey was a member of the audience of a play by Shakespeare in which the playwright made the same observation, but again the feeling that artists never contribute anything to society blocked anyone but Harvey from considering the statement as anything more than fiction.

Finally, Harvey made his announcement. Immediately dead cats, rotten fruit and pieces of wine jugs were hurled in his direction. He raised quite a commotion in medical and social circles until finally, in desperation, one doctor made the historical statement that, "I would rather err with Galen than be right with Harvey!"

Man would have made an advance of exactly zero if this had always been the only method of testing evidence. But every so often during Man's progress, there have been rebels who were not satisfied with preponderance of opinion, and who tested a fact for themselves, observing and accepting the data of their observation, and then testing again.

Possibly the first man who made a flint axe looked over a piece of flint and decided that the irregular stone could be chipped a certain way. When he found that flint would chip easily, he must have rushed to his tribe and enthusiastically tried to teach his fellow tribesmen how to make axes in the shape they desired, instead of spending months searching for accidental pieces of stone of just the right shape. The chances are he was stoned out of camp.

Indulging in a further flight of fancy, it is not difficult to imagine that he finally managed to convince another fellow that his technique worked and that the two of them tied down a third with a piece of vine and forced him to watch them chip a flint axe from a rough stone. Finally, after convincing fifteen or twenty tribesmen by forceful demonstration, the followers of the new technique declared war on the rest of the tribe and, winning, forced the tribe to agree by decree.

Evaluation of Data

Man has never known very much about that with which his mind is chiefly filled: Data. What is data?

126

What is the evaluation of data?

All these years, in which psychoanalysis has taught its tenets to each generation of doctors, the authoritarian method was used, as can be verified by reading a few of the books on the subject. Within them is found, interminably, "Freud said . . . ." The truly important thing is not that "Freud said" a thing, but "Is the data valuable? If it is valuable, how valuable is it?" You might say that a datum is as valuable as it has been evaluated. A datum can be proved in ratio to whether it can be evaluated by other data, and its magnitude is established by how many other data it clarifies. Thus, the biggest datum possible would be one which would clarify and identify all knowledge known to man in the material universe.

Unfortunately, however, there is no such thing as a Prime Datum. There must be, not one datum, but two data, since a datum is of no use unless it can be evaluated. Furthermore, there must be a datum of similar magnitude with which to evaluate any given datum.

Data is your data only so long as you have evaluated it. It is your data by authority or it is your data. If it is your data by authority somebody has forced it upon you, and at best it is little more than a light aberration. Of course, if you asked a question of a man whom you thought knew his business and he gave you his answer, that datum was not forced upon you. But if you went away from him believing from then on that such a datum existed without taking the trouble to investigate the answer for yourself—without comparing it to the known universe—you were falling short of completing the cycle of learning.

Mechanically, the major thing wrong with the mind is, of course, the turbulence in it; but the overburden of information in this society is enforced education that the individual has never been permitted to test. Literally, when you are told not to take anyone's word as an absolute datum, you are being asked to break a habit pattern forced upon you when you were a child.

Test it for yourself and convince yourself whether or not it exists as truth. And if you find that it does exist, you will be comfortable thereafter; otherwise, unrecognized even by yourself, you are likely to find, down at the bottom of your information and education, an unresolved question which will itself undermine your ability to assimilate or practice anything in the line of a technique. Your mind will not be as facile on the subject as it should be.

A Look at the Sciences

The reason engineering and physics have reached out so far in advance of other sciences is the fact that they pose problems which punish man so violently if he doesn't look carefully into the physical universe.

An engineer is faced with the problem of drilling a tunnel through a mountain for a railroad. Tracks are laid up to the mountain on either side. If he judged space wrongly, the two tunnel entrances would fail to meet on the same level in the center. It would be so evident to one and all concerned that the engineer had made a mistake, that he takes great care not to make such a mistake. He observes the physical universe, not only to the extent that the tunnel must meet to a fraction of an inch, but to the extent that, if he were to judge wrongly the character of the rock through which he drills, the tunnel would cave in—an incident which would be considered a very unlucky and unfortunate occurrence to railroading.

Biology comes closer to being a science than some others because, in the field of biology, if someone makes too big a mistake about a bug, the immediate result can be dramatic and terrifying. Suppose a biologist is charged with the responsibility of injecting plankton into a water reservoir. Plankton are microscopic "germs" that are very useful to man.

129

But, if through some mistake, the biologist injects typhoid germs into the water supply—there would be an immediate and dramatic result.

Suppose a biologist is presented with the task of producing a culture of yeast which would, when placed in white bread dough, stain the bread brown. This man is up against the necessity of creating a yeast which not only behaves as yeast, but makes a dye as well. He has to deal with the practical aspect of the problem, because after he announces his success, there is the "yeast test": Is the bread edible? And the brown-bread test: Is the bread brown? Anyone could easily make the test, and everyone would know very quickly whether or not the biologist had succeeded or failed.

Politics is called a science. There are natural laws about politics. They could be worked out if someone were to actually apply a scientific basis to political research.

For instance, it is a foregone conclusion that if all communication lines are cut between the United States and Russia, Russia and the United States are going to understand each other less and less. Then, by demonstrating to everyone how the American way of life and the Russian way of life are different and by demonstrating it day after day, year after year, there is no alternative but a break of affinity. By stating flatly that Russia and the United States are not in agreement on any slightest political theory or conduct of man or nations, the job is practically complete. Both nations will go into anger tone and suddenly, there is war.

The United States is a nation possessed of the greatest communications networks on the face of the earth, with an undreamed-of manufacturing potential. It has within its borders the best advertising men in the world. But instead of selling Europe an idea, it gives machine guns, planes and tanks for use in case Russia breaks out. The more threats imposed against a country in Russia's tone level, the more dangerous that country will become. When people are asked what they would do about this grave question, they shrug and say something to the effect that "the politicians know best." They hedge and rationalize by saying that, after all, there is the American way of life, and it must be protected.

What is the American way of life? This is a question that will stop almost any American. What is the American way of life that is different from the human way of life? It has tried to gather together economic freedom for the individual, freedom of the press, and individual freedom, and define them as a strictly American way of life—why hasn't it been

131

called the Human Way of Life?

In the field of humanities, Science has been thoroughly adrift. Unquestioned authoritarian principles have been followed. Any person who accepts knowledge without questioning it and evaluating it for himself is demonstrating himself to be in apathy toward that sphere of knowledge. It demonstrates that the people in the United States today must be in a low state of apathy with regard to politics, in order to accept, without question, everything that happens.

Fundamentals

When a man tries to erect the plans of a lifetime or a profession on data which he, himself, has never evaluated, he cannot possibly succeed.

Fundamentals are very, very important, but first of all one must learn how to think in order to be absolutely sure of a fundamental. Thinking is not particularly hard to learn. It consists merely of comparing a particular datum with the physical universe as it is known and observed.

Authoritarianism is little more than a form of hypnotism. Learning is forced under threat of some form of punishment. A student is stuffed with data which has not been individually evaluated, just as a taxidermist would stuff a snake. Such a student will be well informed and well educated according to present-day standards, but, unfortunately, he will not be very successful in his chosen profession.

Do not make the mistake of criticizing something on the basis of whether or not it concurs with the opinions of someone else. The point which is pertinent is whether or not it concurs with your opinion. Does it agree with what you think?

Nearly everyone has done some manner of observing of the material universe. No one has seen all there is to see about an organism, for example, but there is certainly no dearth of organisms available for further study. There is no valid reason for accepting the opinion of Professor Blotz of the Blitz University, who said in 1933 that schizophrenics were schizophrenics, and that made them schizophrenics for all time.

If you are interested in the manifestation of insanity, there is any and every form of insanity that you could hope to see in a lifetime in almost any part of the world. Study the peculiarities of the people around you and wonder what they would be like if their little peculiarities were magnified a hundred-fold. You may find that by listing all the observable

133

peculiarities you would have a complete list of all the insanities in the world. This list might well be far more accurate than that which was advanced by Kraepelin and used in the United States today.

If sanity is rationality and insanity is irrationality, and you postulated how irrational people would be if certain of their obsessions were magnified a hundredfold, you might well have in your possession a far more accurate and complete list of insanities and their manifestations than is currently in existence.

So, the only advice I can give to the student is to study a subject for itself and use it exactly as stated, then form his own opinions. Study it with the purpose in mind of arriving at his own conclusions as to whether or not the tenets he has assimilated are correct and workable. Compare what you have learned with the known universe. Seek for the reasons behind a manifestation, and postulate the manner and in which direction the manifestation will likely proceed. Do not allow the Authority of any one person or school of thought to create a foregone conclusion within your sphere of knowledge. Only with these principles of education in mind can you become a truly educated individual.

THE HUMAN MIND

It is common to think of the human mind as
something which just happened in the last generation or so. The mind itself is actually as old as the
organism. And according to earlier guesses and
proofs established by this new science, the organism,
the body, is rather old. It goes back to the first
moment of Life's appearance on Earth.

First, there was a physical universe which
happened, we know not how. And then, with the
cooling planets, there appeared in the seas a speck of
living matter. That speck became eventually the
complicated but still microscopic monocell. And
then, as the eons passed, it became vegetable matter.
And then it became jellyfish. And then it became a
mollusk and made its transition into crustacea. Life
evolved into more and more complex forms, the
tarsus, the sloth, the anthropoid, and finally Man.
There were many intermediate steps.

A very materialistic Man, seeing only the material
universe, becomes confused and vague about all this.
He tries to say that living organisms are simply so

135

much clay, wholly a part of the material universe. He tries to say that after all it is only the "unending stream of protoplasm", generation to generation by sex that is important. The very unthinking Man is likely to make many mistakes, not only about the human mind, but the human body.

We discover now that the science of life, like physics, is a study of statics and motion. We find that Life itself, the living part of Life, has no comparable entity in the physical universe. It isn't just another energy or just an accident. Life is a static which yet has the power of controlling, animating, mobilizing, organizing and destroying matter, energy and space and possibly even time.

Life is a CAUSE which acts upon the physical universe as an EFFECT. There is overwhelming evidence to support this now. In the physical universe there is no true static. Every apparent static has been discovered to contain motion. But the static of Life is evidently a true static.

Life began with pure CAUSE evidently. With the first photon it engaged in handling motion. And by handling motion ever afterwards, accumulated the experience and effort contained in a body. Life is a static, the physical universe is motion. The effect upon motion of CAUSE produced the combination

136

which we see as the unity of a live organism. Thought is not motion in space and time. Thought is a static containing an image of motion.

Thus, one can say, with its first impingement upon motion, the first thought about the physical universe began. This static, without volume, wave length, space or time, yet records motion and its effects in space and time.

This is, of course, analogy. But it is a peculiar analogy, in that it sweepingly resolves the problems of mind and physical structure.

A mind, then, is not a brain. A brain and the nervous system are simply conduits for physical universe vibrations. The brain and nerve trunks are much like a switchboard system. And there is a point in the system where the vibrations change into records.

An organism is motivated by continuing, timeless, spaceless, motionless CAUSE. This cause mirrors or takes impressions of motion. These impressions we call "memories" or more accurately, *facsimiles*.

A *facsimile* is a simple word meaning a picture of a thing, a copy of a thing, not the thing itself. Thus, to save confusion and keep this point before us, we

137

say that the perceptions of the body are "stored" as facsimiles.

Sights, sounds, tastes, and all the other perceptions of the body store as facsimiles of the moment the impression was received. The actual energy of the impression is not stored. It is not stored, if only because there is insufficient molecular structure in the body to store these energies as such. Physical universe energy is evidently too gross for such storage. Further, although the cells perish, the memories go on, existing, evidently, forever.

A facsimile of yesterday's hurt toe can be brought back today with the full force of the impact. Everything which occurs around the body, whether it is asleep or awake, is recorded as a facsimile and is stored.

There are facsimiles of anything and everything the body has ever perceived—seen, heard, felt, smelled, tasted, experienced—from the first moment of existence. There are pleasure facsimiles and bored facsimiles, facsimiles of sudden death and quick success, facsimiles of quiet decay and gradual struggle.

Memory usually means recalling data of recent times; thus we use the word "facsimile", for while it is the whole of which memory is a part, the word "memory" does not embrace all that has been discovered.

One should have a very good idea of what a facsimile is. It is a recording of the motions and situations of the physical universe plus the conclusions of the mind based on earlier facsimiles.

One sees a dog chase a cat. Long after dog and cat are gone one can recall that a dog chased a cat. While the action was taking place one saw the scene, one heard the sounds, one might even smell the dog or cat. As one watched, his own heart was beating, the saline content of his blood was at such and such a point, the weight of one's body and the position of one's joints, the feel of one's clothing, the touch of the air upon the skin, all these things were recorded in full as well. The total of all this would be a unit facsimile.

Now one could simply recall the fact that one had seen a dog chase a cat. That would be remembering. Or one could concentrate on the matter and, if he was in good mental condition, could again see the dog and the cat, could hear them, could feel the air on his skin, the position of his joints, the weight of his clothing. He could partially or wholly regain the experience. That is to say, he could partially or

139

wholly bring to his consciousness the "memory", the unit facsimile of a dog chasing a cat.

One does not have to be drugged or hypnotized or have faith in order to do this. People do variations of this recall and suppose that "everybody does it". The person with a good memory is only a person who can regain his facsimiles easily. A little child in school learns, today, by repetition. It isn't necessary. If he gets good grades it is usually because he simply brings back "to mind", which is to say, to his awareness, the facsimile of the page of text on which he is being examined.

As one goes through life, he records twenty-four hours a day, asleep and awake, in pain, under anaesthetic, happy or sad. These facsimiles are usually recorded with all perceptics, which is to say, with every sense channel. In the person who has a missing sense channel, such as deafness, that portion of the facsimile is missing.

A full facsimile is a sort of three-dimensional color picture with sound and smell and all other perceptions plus the conclusions or speculations of the individual.

It was once, many years ago, noticed by a student of the mind that children had this faculty of seeing

140

and hearing in memory what they had actually seen and heard. And it was noted that the ability did not last. No further study was made of the matter and indeed, so obscure were these studies that I did not know about them during the early stages of my own work.

We know a great deal about these facsimiles now—why they are not easily recovered by most people when they grow up, how they change, how the imagination can begin to re-manufacture them, as in hallucination or dreaming.

Briefly, a person is as aberrated as he is unable to handle his facsimiles. He is as sane as he can handle his facsimiles. He is as ill as he is unable to handle his facsimiles. He is as well as he can handle them.

That portion of the science of Scientology which is devoted to the rehabilitation of the mind and body deals with the phenomena of handling these facsimiles.

A person ought to be able to pick up and inspect and lay aside at will any facsimile he has. It is not a goal of this new science to restore full recall perception; it is the goal to rehabilitate the ability of a person to handle his facsimiles.

When a person CANNOT handle his facsimiles, he can pull them into present time and discover himself unable to get rid of them again.

What is psychosomatic illness? Demonstrably, it is the pain contained in a past experience or the physical malfunction of a past experience. The facsimile of that experience gets into present time and stays with the person until a shock drops it out of sight again or until it is processed out by this new science. A shock or necessity, however, permits it to come back.

Grief, sorrow, worry, anxiety and any other emotional condition is simply one or more of these facsimiles. A circumstance of death, let us say, causes one to grieve. Then one has a facsimile containing grief. Something causes the individual to bring that facsimile into present time. He is unaware of it, is not inspecting it, but it acts against him nevertheless. Thus he is grieving in present time and does not know why. The reason is the old facsimile. The proof that it is the reason lies in Scientology processing. The instant the facsimile is discharged of its painful emotion, the individual recovers. This is processing in one of its phases.

The human mind is only a phase of the continuing mind. The first spark of life which began animating

142

matter upon Earth began recording facsimiles. And it recorded from there on out. It is interesting that the entire file is available to any mind. In previous investigations I occasionally found facsimiles, which were not hallucination or imagination, which seemed to go back much earlier than the present life of the individual. Having by then the tool of effort processing*, it was possible to "turn on" a facsimile with all perceptics at will and so it was possible to examine the earliest periods possible. The genetic blueprint was thus discovered and I was startled to have laid bare, accessible to any future investigator, the facsimiles of the evolutionary line. Many Auditors have since accomplished the same results and thus the biologist and anthropologist come into possession of a mine of fascinating data.

There are those who know nothing of the mind and yet who get amply paid for it who will talk wisely about illusion and delusion. There happen to be exact and precise laws to delusion. An imaginary incident follows certain patterns. An actual incident is entirely unmistakable. There is a standard behavior in a facsimile of an actual experience: It behaves in a certain way; the individual gets the efforts and perceptions with clarity and the content of the incident expands and remains fairly constant

*effort processing. A specific Scientology process in which various basic efforts of the individual are addressed; i.e., the effort to see.

on several recountings. An imaginary incident contracts in content ordinarily and the individual seeks to keep up his interest then by embroidering it. Further, it has no constant efforts in it. Those who cannot take time to establish the actuality of facsimiles before becoming wise about "delusion" are themselves possibly quite delusory people.

The human mind, as the present mind of Man, differs not at all from the most elementary of minds, that of the monocell, except in the complexity of brain appendage. The human being is using facsimiles to evaluate experience and form conclusions and future plans on how to survive in the best possible manner or how to die and start over again.

The human mind is capable of very complex combinations of facsimiles. Further, it can originate facsimiles on the basis of old facsimiles. Nothing goes wrong with the mind except its abilities to handle facsimiles. Occasionally a mind becomes incapable of using a facsimile as past experience and begins to use it in present time continually as an apology for failure. Then we have aberration and psychosomatic illness. A memory of pain contains pain and can become present time pain. A memory of emotion contains emotion and can become present time emotion.

144

RECORDS OF THE MIND ARE PERMANENT

Man for all his years took the observation for the fact that, when a human being was no longer able to control its own operations and functions and, so long as it, again in control, could not recall what had occurred, the material was not recorded. This was wholly unwarranted as an assumption.

Let us examine, first, pain. Pain, technically, is caused by an effort counter to the effort of the individual as a whole.

The individual is a colonial aggregation of cells. Each cell is seeking to live. Each cell and the whole organism is basically motivated by a desire to survive.

The entire physical structure is composed of atoms and molecules, organic and inorganic. While the individual is alive and conscious, these atoms and molecules are in a state of optimum or near-optimum tension and alignment.

On the receipt of a counter effort, such as that of a

blow, or, internally, as in the case of drugs, shock or bacteria, the optimum or near-optimum tension and alignment of these atoms and molecules, as contained in the nerves, muscles, bones and tissues of the body, are disarranged. The result is a slackening or speeding of the motions of the physical body in such a way as to cause misalignment and maltension of the atoms and molecules.

This is pain. Counter-efforts to survival cause this effect to take place. The technical name of this effect is randomity*. The directions of motion of the various portions of the body are disarranged into random vectors or patterns. Pain results in loss, invariably, the loss of cells or the loss of general alignment.

When pain departs, it is still on record. The record of that pain can be called again into existence.

If you wish to make a very simple test, simply go back to the last time you hurt yourself. Get as full perceptions as you can of the object which hurt you and the surrounding environment. Seek to contact the painful object again. Unless you are badly occluded**, you should be able to feel that pain

*randomity. The ratio of unpredicted motion to predicted motion.
**occluded. Memory not available for recall. Someone who is occluded has a poor memory and poor recalls of the past.

146

once more. If you, yourself, cannot make this test because you are occluded, ask your friends to try it. Sooner or later you will find someone who can recall pain.

Another test: Pinch yourself and then go back to the moment you did it and feel the pinch again. Even if you are occluded, you should be able to do this.

In short, pain is stored on record. But that is not all that is stored. The whole area of any randomity is stored in full. The atoms and molecules rearrange themselves, when pain is recontacted, into the pattern they had when that pain was received. Hence, the pain can come back. But also the effort and all of its perceptions can come back when either the pain or the general randomity come back.

The misalignment caused by a blow, shock, drugs, or bacteria causes an inability of the control center of the mind to function. Thus, the control center of the mind can go unconscious, can be overwhelmed by this misalignment.

After consciousness is regained, whenever the control center of the mind tries to recall what happened, it can recall only the randomity. It is trying to recall a time when it could not recall and, thus, draws a blank.

147

Man thought that if he could not recall a thing, then it didn't record. This is like the little child who hides his eyes and then thinks you can't see him just because he can't see you.

With every area of randomity thus created by injury or illness or shock or drugs, there is stored, as well, the counter effort to the body. The effort impinged upon the body by the blow or the other misaligning factor also was stored. This is physical force. When it comes back upon the body, it comes back as physical force. It can distort features or the body by being in constant "restimulation".

Restimulation is occasioned by some part of the early recording being approximated in the environment in the present. This calls up the old area of randomity. The body, confused, registers the old counter-effort.

Nearly everyone has these counter-efforts of the past being, some of them, exerted against him in the present. His sub-level awareness is tied up in resisting old counter-efforts—blows, sicknesses, drugs—which once affected him and drove him into unconsciousness.

The moment an individual wholly concentrates his attention elsewhere, these old areas may exert their force again.

Feel the aliveness or full sense of being of each one of the following. Feel wholly alive only in the member of your body named:

1. The right foot.
2. The left foot.
3. The right cheek.
4. The left cheek.
5. The toes.
6. The back of the head.
7. The back of the neck.
8. The nose.
9. The right hand.
10. The tongue.
11. The left hand.
12. The stomach.

If you have gone over these members, investing carefully, aliveness only in each, you probably will have received various aches and pains in areas where your concentration was not fixed or at least, experienced grogginess. Try it several times.

Processing cleans up these old areas with resultant rise in health and sanity.

COMMUNICATION

It could be said that if you would get a person into communication you would get him well. This factor is not new in psychotherapy, but concentration upon it is new, and interpretation of ability as communication is entirely new.

If you were to be in thorough and complete communication with a car on a road, you would certainly have no difficulty driving that car. But if you were in only partial communication with the car and in no communication with the road, it is fairly certain that an accident would occur. Most accidents do occur when the driver is distracted by an argument he has had, or by an arrest, or by a cross alongside of the road that says where some motorist got killed, or by his own fears of accidents.

When we say that somebody should be in present time we mean he should be in communication with his environment. We mean, further, that he should be in communication with his environment as it exists, not as it existed. And when we speak of prediction, we mean that he should be in communication with his environment as it will exist, as well as as it exists.

If communication is so important, what is communication? It is best expressed as its formula, which has been isolated, and by use of which a great many interesting results can be brought about in ability changes. The formula of Communication is: Cause, Distance, Effect, with Intention, Attention and Duplication.

There are two kinds of communication, both depending upon the viewpoint assumed. There is outflowing communication and inflowing communication. A person who is talking to somebody else is communicating to that person (we trust), and the person being talked to is receiving communication from that person. Now, as the conversation changes, we find that the person who has been talked to is now doing the talking and is talking to the first person, who is now receiving communication from him.

A conversation is the process of alternating outflowing and inflowing communication, and right here exists the oddity which makes aberration and entrapment. There is a basic rule here: He who would outflow must also inflow—he who would inflow must also outflow. When we find this rule

151

overbalanced in either direction, we discover difficulty. A person who is only outflowing communication is actually not communicating at all in the fullest sense of the word, for in order to communicate entirely he would have to inflow as well as outflow. A person who is inflowing communication entirely is again out of order, for if he would inflow he must then outflow.

Any and all objections anyone has to social and human relationships is to be found basically in this rule of communication, where it is disobeyed. Anyone who is talking, if he is not in a compulsive or obsessive state of beingness, is dismayed when he does not get answers. Similarly, anyone who is being talked to is dismayed when he is not given an opportunity to give his reply.

Even hypnotism can be understood by this rule of communication. Hypnotism is a continuing inflow without an opportunity on the part of the subject to outflow. This is carried on to such a degree in hypnotism that the individual is actually trapped in the spot where he is being hypnotized and will remain trapped in that spot to some degree from there on.

Thus, one might go so far as to say that a bullet's arrival is a heavy sort of hypnotism. The individual

152

receiving a bullet does not outflow a bullet, and thus he is injured. If he could outflow a bullet immediately after receiving a bullet, we could introduce the interesting question, "Would he be wounded?" According to our rule, he would not be. Indeed, if he were in perfect communication with his environment, he could not even receive a bullet injuriously.

An unfinished cycle of communication generates what might be called "answer hunger". An individual who is waiting for a signal that his communication has been received is prone to accept any inflow. When an individual has, for a very long time, consistently waited for answers which did not arrive, any sort of answer from anywhere will be pulled in to him, by him, as an effort to remedy his scarcity of answers.

We have seen an entire race of philosophers go out of existence since 1790. We have seen philosophy become a very unimportant subject, where once it was a very common coin amongst the people. The philosophers, themselves, put themselves out of communication with the people by insisting upon using words of special definitions which could not be assimilated with readiness by persons in general. The currency of philosophy could not be duplicated readily by those with relatively limited vocabularies. Take such jaw-cracking words as "telekinesis"*. While it probably means something very interesting and very vital, if you will think back carefully, no taxi-driver mentioned this word to you while you were paying your fare or even during the more verbose moments of the ride. Probably the basic trouble with philosophy was that it became Germanic in its grammar, an example set by Immanuel Kant. And if you will recall that wonderful story by Saki, a man was once trampled to death while trying to teach an elephant German irregular verbs. Philosophy shed some of its responsibility for a cycle of communication by rendering itself unduplicatable by its readers. It is the responsibility of anyone who would communicate that he speak with such vocabulary as can be understood.

Now, let us take up the individual who has become very "experienced" in life. This individual has a time-track**, it isn't anyone else's time-track. The basic individualities amongst men are based upon the fact that they have different things happen to them and that they view these different things from different points of view. Thus, we have individualization and we have individual opinion, consideration and experience.

*telekinesis. The production of motion at a distance by means beyond the range of the senses.
**time-track. The entire record, complete with all perceptions, of the individual's existence in the physical universe.

Two men walking down the street witness an accident. Each one of them sees the accident from at least a slightly different point of view. Consulting twelve different witnesses to the same accident, we are likely to find twelve different accidents. Completely aside from the fact that witnesses like to tell you what they think they saw instead of what they saw, there were actually twelve different points from which the accident was viewed and so twelve different aspects of the occurrences. If these twelve were brought together and if they were to communicate amongst themselves about this accident, they would then reach a point of agreement on what actually happened. This might not have been the accident, but it certainly is the agreed-upon accident, which then becomes the real accident. This is the way juries conduct themselves. They might or might not be passing upon the real crime, but they are certainly passing upon the agreed-upon crime.

In any war, it takes two or three days for enough agreement to occur to know what took place in a battle. Whereas there might have been a real battle, a real sequence of incidents and occurrences, the fact that every man in the battle saw the battle from his own particular point of view, by which we mean severely "point from which he was looking", rather than his opinions—no one saw the battle in its entirety. Thus, time must intervene for enough

155

communication on the subject of the battle to take place so that all have some semblance of agreement on what occurred.

Of course, when the historians get to this battle and start writing different accounts of it, out of the memoirs of generals who were trying to explain away their defeats, we get a highly distorted account, indeed. And yet this becomes the agreed-upon battle, as far as history is concerned. Reading the historians one realizes that one will never really know what took place at Waterloo, at Bennington, at Marathon. In that we can consider as a communication one soldier shooting at another soldier, we see that we are studying communications about communication.

Now we come to the problem of what a life unit must be willing to experience in order to communicate. In the first place the primary cause point must be willing to be duplicatable. It must be able to give at least some attention to the receipt point. The primary receipt point must be willing to duplicate, must be willing to receive, and must be willing to change into a source point in order to send the communication, or an answer to it, back. And the primary source point in its turn must be willing to be a receipt point.

As we are dealing basically with ideas and not mechanics, we see then that a state of mind must exist between a cause and effect point whereby each one is willing to be Cause or Effect at will and is willing to duplicate at will, is willing to be duplicatable at will, is willing to change at will, is willing to experience the distance between, and, in short, willing to communicate.

Where we get these conditions in an individual or a group, we have sane people. Where an unwillingness to send or receive communications occurs, where people obsessively or compulsively send communications without direction and without trying to be duplicatable, where individuals in receipt of communications stand silent and do not acknowledge or reply, we have aberrative factors.

A man is as dead as he cannot communicate. He is as alive as he can communicate. With countless tests I have discovered, to a degree which could be called conclusive, that the only remedy for livingness is further communicatingness. One must add to his ability to communicate.

For a great many years I asked this question, "To communicate or not to communicate?" If one got himself into such thorough trouble by communicating, then, of course, one should stop com-

157

municating. But this is not the case. If one gets himself into trouble by communicating, he should further communicate. More communication, not less, is the answer, and I consider this riddle solved after a quarter-century of investigation and pondering.

Dianetics Books
By L. Ron Hubbard

Dianetics: The Original Thesis

A scholarly work, written by L. Ron Hubbard in early 1948, to present the basic causes of human behavior and the resolution of mental aberration and psychosomatic illness to the medical and psychiatric societies. It is a fascinating account, but more importantly, in this text Ron makes his original and perhaps most basic statement of those timeless truths which dispel man's ignorance.

Dianetics: The Evolution of a Science

Is man, as most psychologists hold, a primitive animal whose basic savage nature is held in check only by rigid social conditioning, or is his basic nature good, creative and constructive? The answer was looked for and found! With this book, follow the research track of how Ron evolved Dianetics.

Dianetics: The Modern Science of Mental Health

Published in May 1950, *Dianetics* shot to the top of the best seller lists across the country and stayed there week after week and month after month—and has been a continuing best seller of international importance ever since. World response to *Dianetics* was typically expressed in terms like those appearing in the *New York Times* in August 1950. "As with all great books, the impact of *Dianetics* means the world will never be the same again. History has become a race between Dianetics and catastrophe. Dianetics will win if enough people are challenged, in time, to understand it."

Notes on the Lectures

Taken from the 1950 Los Angeles and Oakland lecture series, this book explains the relationship between the physical universe and the universe of thought. Two different universes. If you want to know more about people and why they are what they are, then study this book.

Child Dianetics

(Taken from the works of L. Ron Hubbard.)
Have you all but given up on handling children? Parents who read *Child Dianetics* and give its simple exercises to their children will find out that something can be done!

Science of Survival

Written about a remarkable chart: The Hubbard Chart of Human Evaluation. With this chart you will be able to predict human behavior.

Advanced Procedure and Axioms

Advanced Dianetic discoveries and techniques comprising a research breakthrough by L. Ron Hubbard beyond the field of the mind into codification of the basic principles of existence. Contains over 200 definitions, logics and axioms of Dianetics.

Self Analysis

Contains exercises which can be used by anyone to better his life. Unlock a stronger more confident "you" simply by reliving past pleasures you've enjoyed. A proven system that's so easy you won't believe it works—until you try it.

Dianetics 55!

In this book, L. Ron Hubbard deals with the problems and fundamental principles of communication between man and man, and between man and his environment.

The Basic Dianetics Picture Book

A visual aid for a quicker understanding and dissemination of Standard Dianetics and Dianetic processing.

Dianetics Today

Published in 1975, this book details the developments by L. Ron Hubbard in Dianetics 25 years after *Dianetics: The Modern Science of Mental Health* was first released.

Research and Discovery Series

There are about 25,000,000 words of taped lectures in archives which contain the consecutive path of discovery made by L. Ron Hubbard. These tapes are not simply lectures. They are the only record of all the advances which made possible the handling of the human mind. They are being transcribed into a 75-100 volume set. The first few big beautiful volumes are published. They are the beginning of the running record of research into the mind and life. The Research and Discovery Series is a must for active Dianetic Auditors.

Order these books direct from the publisher:
Write for your free price list:

Bridge Publications, Inc.
1414 North Catalina Street
Los Angeles, California 90027-9990

Scientology Books
By L. Ron Hubbard

Basic Books

The Basic Scientology Picture Book

(Taken from the works of L. Ron Hubbard.)
Basic Scientology is described through pictures, drawings, simple diagrams and text in a large easy-to-read format.

Scientology: The Fundamentals of Thought

What has been attempted by a thousand universities and foundations at a cost of billions has been accomplished quietly here. Give this book to a man or woman in trouble, a man or woman with an inquiring nature, and let that man or woman study this volume carefully and apply it.

A New Slant on Life

Twenty-eight all-time favorite essays by the Founder of Scientology are brought together in an enjoyable and profoundly useful volume.

The Problems of Work

How to relieve exhaustion, ease stress of working relationships, increase efficiency, find greater satisfaction and success. This simple book can help make work a lot more fun!

What Is Scientology?

(Based on the works of L. Ron Hubbard)
Contains facts, statistics, Scientology history, important dates, publications, social programs, and more. Illustrated with over 100 color photographs, 36 paintings, charts, tables and other illustrations.

Scientology 0-8: The Book of Basics

Contains the basic axioms, scales and charts of Scientology and Dianetics. A concise collection of data which form the philosophical basis of these two subjects. An extremely usable book.

Axioms and Logics

A concise booklet containing the Axioms of Scientology, the Prelogics, the Logics, the Axioms of Dianetics.

Handbooks

Handbook for Preclears
Written by Ron in 1951 to meet the demand for a personal workbook, a good sound text that anyone could pick up, learn, and follow in easily done steps to gain changes in the conditions of their lives. Designed for use as a self-help volume, and for use by the trained auditor and intelligent layman.

The Volunteer Minister's Handbook
Specially designed for people who want to learn how to help others, it is broken down into 21 sections, each covering an aspect of life, with a checksheet for each section. *Anyone* can become a Volunteer Minister and help handle such situations as: broken marriages, accidents, drug or alcohol problems, difficult children, and more.

Specialized Subjects

All About Radiation
Gives a fascinating summary of facts and figures concerning the effects of radiation mentally and physically. It clears up for the caring individual, the worldwide controversy and mystery on the subject.

Have You Lived Before This Life?
Forty-one personal accounts of what it's really like to recall a past life and how this awareness has changed people's lives. An exciting book that you won't be able to put down!

Introduction to Scientology Ethics
In this system will be found the way to true justice and a workable system of ethics for this planet.

How to Live Though an Executive
The solutions to the problems of the modern business are summarized by L. Ron Hubbard in this book. Based on years of research into many different types of organizations.

Mission Into Time
What happens when L. Ron Hubbard puts his memory of personal past life experiences to the test? You'll find out when you read this fascinating book!

Advanced Texts

Scientology: A History of Man
"This is a cold-blooded and factual account of your last sixty trillion years."

Scientology 8–80
This book documents a major research breakthrough, and contains the factors necessary to rehabilitate life energy and thereby give its control back to the individual.

Scientology 8–8008
First released in 1952 to attendees of the Philadelphia Doctorate Course, this unique volume contains Ron's early research into the spirit of Man—its true nature, abilities and relationship to the physical universe.

The Creation of Human Ability
This history-making book of 1954 giving the Axioms of Scientology, the Codes, The Factors, and a huge number of processes for use by Scientology auditors.

The Phoenix Lectures
Covers many facets of Scientology. In it Ron traces the philosophical roots of Scientology from the Vedic writings of ancient India, through Middle Eastern and Western thought, to the present day. An extremely important book.

The E-Meter

The Book Introducing the E-Meter
A book of basic drills by L. Ron Hubbard which gives the beginner his first familiarization with the use of the Hubbard Electrometer. Photo illustrated throughout.

The Book of E-Meter Drills
"This booklet contains all the standard E-Meter drills used in training in Scientology. There are no other drills. Many have been developed from time to time and have proven less workable and useless. These drills have been of the greatest possible value."—L. Ron Hubbard

Understanding the E-Meter
A simple, elementary text which shows exactly how the E-Meter works. Vital to understanding the E-Meter. Fully illustrated.

E-Meter Essentials

A standard text for all Dianetics and Scientology training on the use of the E-Meter. Written in an easy style, this book is loaded with solid know-how every student needs to master.

Administrative Technology

The Organization Executive Course

The Organization Executive Course Volumes are eight big encyclopedia-size volumes containing L. Ron Hubbard's incredibly workable organizing technology—the "how to" of running *any* post or job or organization.

How to survive in today's world of job scarcity, rising prices and material shortages is a question many people are asking. Scientology churches all over the world are not only surviving, but *expanding*. The answer to what makes this "impossible" feat possible is contained in these volumes.

Management Series

The most advanced management technology ever discovered. Based on many years of first hand experience with organizations across the world and an intense study of organizations that rose and fell throughout history. This is a fine distillation of what *works*. Vital knowledge for any executive at any level. Fully indexed.

Modern Management Technology Defined

An unabridged dictionary of 6600 Scientology administrative terms with an additional 2000 non-Scientology business terms. Contains 8600 entries, 13,200 definitions and is the perfect complement to the Organization Executive Course and Management Series Volumes.

Scientology and Dianetics Technology

The Book Of Case Remedies

A manual covering preclear difficulties and their remedy for use by Scientology auditors in counselling, Supervisors running courses, and any Scientologiest who wishes to help another along the road.

Control and the Mechanics of Start–Change–Stop

Control is not popular in today's societies. This booklet defines control and explains why it is not popular. It gives simple exercises designed to handle bad reactions to control and raise a person's ability to handle control on his own determinism. An excellent manual for anyone at all involved in handling people.

Scientology: Clear Procedure

In 1957 Ron wrote "I have been at work for seven years to produce a series of techniques which any well-trained auditor can use to clear people. We now have them." These earlier breakthroughs into Scientology Clearing are published in this booklet.

The Dianetics and Scientology Technical Volumes

These are twelve big volumes, containing all of Ron's technical bulletins from 1950 to 1979. The issues included are Hubbard Communications Office Bulletins (HCOBs), and every early technical issue type—Dianetic Auditor's Bulletins, Hubbard Dianetic Research Foundation Bulletins, Professional Auditor's Bulletins (PABs), Associate Newsletters, Journals of Scientology and articles from Ability magazines and more. *Every question you have ever had concerning the technology of Scientology and Dianetics can be answered through the pages of this set.*

The Dianetics and Scientology Technical Dictionary

An unabridged dictionary of technical terms used in Dianetics and Scientology. Five years in compilation, it contains over 3,000 words with more than 7,000 definitions. Illustrated with drawings and photographs.

Order these books direct from the publisher.
Write for your free price list:

Bridge Pubications, Inc.
1414 North Catalina Street
Los Angeles, California 90027-9990

Contact Your Nearest
Church or Organization

Flag Land Base
Advanced Organizations
Saint Hill Organizations
Publications Organizations

UNITED STATES
OF AMERICA

Church of Scientology
Flag Service Organization
210 South Fort Harrison Avenue
Clearwater, Florida 33516

Church of Scientology of California
Advanced Organization of Los Angeles
1306 North Berendo Street
Los Angeles, California 90027

Church of Scientology of California
American Saint Hill Organization
1413 North Berendo Street
Los Angeles, California 90027

Church of Scientology of California
American Saint Hill Foundation
1413 North Berendo Street
Los Angeles, California 90027

Bridge Publications, Inc.
1414 North Catalina Street
Los Angeles, California 90027

UNITED
KINGDOM

Apollo Advanced Organization
Saint Hill
Saint Hill Manor, East Grinstead
West Sussex, RH19 4JY England

EUROPE

Church of Scientology
Advanced Organization Europe
Jernbanegade 6
1608 Copenhagen V, Denmark

Church of Scientology
Saint Hill Organization Europe
Jernbanegade 6
1608 Copenhagen V, Denmark

New Era Publications ApS
Store Kongensgade 55
1264 Copenhagen K, Denmark

Publicaciones Dianeticas
Alabama No 105
México 18, D.F., México

Churches

WESTERN
UNITED STATES

Church of Scientology
of New Mexico
2712 Carlisle Boulevard N.E.
Albuquerque, New Mexico 87110

Church of Scientology of Texas
2200 Guadalupe
Austin, Texas 78705

Church of Scientology of Colorado
375 South Navajo Street
Denver, Colorado 80223

Church of Scientology of Hawaii
447 Nahua Street
Honolulu, Hawaii 96815

Church of Scientology Kansas City
1206 West 39th Street
Kansas City, Missouri 64111

Church of Scientology of Nevada
846 East Sahara Avenue
Las Vegas, Nevada 89104

Church of Scientology of Los Angeles
4810 Sunset Boulevard
Los Angeles, California 90027

Church of Scientology of Minnesota
900 Hennepin Avenue
Minneapolis, Minnesota 55403

Church of Scientology Pasadena
99 East Colorado Boulevard
Pasadena, California 91105

Church of Scientology of Arizona
4450 North Central Avenue
Phoenix, Arizona 85014

Church of Scientology of Portland
215 South East 9th Avenue
Portland, Oregon 97214

Church of Scientology of Sacramento
825 15th Street
Sacramento, California 95814-2096

Church of Scientology of San Diego
348 Olive
San Diego, California 92103

Church of Scientology
of San Francisco
83-91 McAllister Street
San Francisco, California 94102

Church of Scientology Santa Barbara
20 West De la Guerra
Santa Barbara, California 93101

Chruch of Scientology
of Washington State
1318 Second Avenue
Seattle, Washington 98101

Church of Scientology
San Fernando Valley
13561 Ventura Boulevard
Sherman Oaks, California 91403

Church of Scientology of Missouri
3730 Lindell Boulevard
Saint Louis, Missouri 63108

EASTERN
UNITED STATES

Church of Scientology of Boston
448 Beacon Street
Boston, Massachusetts 02115

Church of Scientology Buffalo
47 West Huron Street
Buffalo, New York 14202

Church of Scientology of Ohio
3352 Jefferson Avenue
Cincinnati, Ohio 45220

Church of Scientology
of Central Ohio
167 East State Street
Columbus, Ohio 43215

Church of Scientology of Florida
120 Giralda Avenue
Coral Gables, Florida 33134

Church of Scientology of Michigan
751 Griswold
Detroit, Michigan 48226

Church of Scientology of Illinois
845 Chicago Avenue
Evanston, Illinois 60202

Church of Scientology of Long Island
46 Islip Avenue
Islip, New York 11751

Church of Scientology of New Haven
909 Whalley Avenue
New Haven, Connecticut 06515

Church of Scientology of New York
227 West 46th Street
New York City, New York 10036

Church of Scientology of Orlando
111 East Robinson Street
Orlando, Florida 32801

Church of Scientology
of Pennsylvania
1315-17 Race Street
Philadelphia, Pennsylvania 19107

Church of Scientology of Tampa
436 West Kennedy Boulevard
Tampa, Florida 33606

Church of Scientology
of Washington, D.C.
2125 ''S'' Street N.W.
Washington, D.C. 20008

CANADA

Church of Scientology of Alberta
10349 82nd Avenue
Edmonton, Alberta
Canada T6E 1Z9

Church of Scientology of Kitchener
8 Water Street North
Kitchener, Ontario
Canada N2H 5A5

Church of Scientology of Montréal
4489 Papineau Street
Montréal, Québec
Canada H2H 1T7

Church of Scientology of Ottawa
309 Cooper Street, 4th Floor
Ottawa, Ontario
Canada K2P 0G5

Church of Scientology of Québec
224-1/2 St-Joseph esl
Québec City, Québec
Canada M4Y 2A7

Church of Scientology of Toronto
696 Yonge Street
Toronto, Ontario
Canada M4Y 2A7

Church of Scientology
of Vancouver
401 West Hastings Street
Vancouver, British Columbia
Canada V6B 1L5

Church of Scientology
of Winnipeg
689 St. Mary's Road
Winnipeg, Manitoba
Canada R2M 3M8

UNITED
KINGDOM

Saint Hill Foundation
Saint Hill Manor
East Grinstead
West Sussex, England RH19 4JY

Scientology Birmingham
3 St. Mary's Row
Moseley, Birmingham
England B13 8HW

Church of Scientology in London
68 Tottenham Court Road
London, England W1E 4YZ

Church of Scientology Manchester
258/260 Deansgate
Manchester, England M3 4BG

Church of Scientology in Plymouth
41 Ebrington Street
Plymouth, Devon
England PL4 9AA

Scientology Sunderland
211 High Street West
Sunderland, Tyne and Wear
England SR1 1UA

Hubbard Academy of Personal
Independence
20 Southbridge
Edinburgh, Scotland EH1 1LL

AUSTRIA

Church of Scientology Vienna
(Scientology-Osterreich)
Mariahilferstrasse 88A/II/2
A-1070 Vienna, Austria

BELGIUM

Church of Scientology Bruxelles
45A, rue de l'Ecuyer
1000 Bruxelles, Belgium

DENMARK

Church of Scientology Jylland
Söndergade 70, 1th
8000 Aarhus C., Denmark

Church of Scientology Copenhagen
Store Kongensgade 55
1264 Copenhagen K, Denmark

Church of Scientology Denmark
Vesterbrogade 23
1620 Copenhagen V, Denmark

FRANCE

Church of Scientology Angers
10, rue Max Richard
49002 Angers Cedex, France

Church of Scientology
Clermont-Ferrand
18, rue André Moinier
63000 Clermont-Ferrand, France

Church of Scientology Lyon
Chemin du Pont aux Biches
69250 Neuville/Saône, France

Church of Scientology de Paris
12, rue de la Montagne
Sainte Geneviève
75005 Paris, France

Church of Scientology St. Etienne
10, rue de la Paix
42000 St Etienne, France

GERMANY

Church of Scientology Berlin
HSO Berlin e.V.
Jagowstrasse 15
D-1000 Berlin 21, Germany

Church of Scientology Munich
Beichstrasse 12
D-8000 Munich 40, West Germany

NETHERLANDS

Church of Scientology Amsterdam
Nieuwe Zijds Voorburgwal 312
1012 RV Amsterdam, Netherlands

NORWAY

Church of Scientology Oslo
Stenersgaten 16
Oslo 1, Norway

SWEDEN

Church of Scientology Götenborg
Kungsgatan 23
S-411 19 Göteborg, Sweden

Scientology Malmö
Stortorget 27-29
S-211-34 Malmö, Sweden

Church of Scientology Stockholm
Kammakargatan 46
S-111-60 Stockholm, Sweden

SWITZERLAND

Church of Scientology Basel
Gundelingerstrasse 432
4053 Basel, Switzerland

Church of Scientology Bern
Effingerstrasse 25
3008 Bern, Switzerland

Church of Scientology Genève
4, rue du Léman
1201 Geneva, Switzerland

**AUSTRALIA
AND NEW ZEALAND**

Church of Scientology A.C.T.
23 East Row, Rooms 2 & 3
Civic, Canberra, A.C.T. Australia 2601

Church of Scientology Adelaide
28 Waymouth Street
Adelaide, South Australia 5000

Church of Scientology Brisbane
64 Tait Street
Brisbane, Queensland, Australia 4059

Church of Scientology Melbourne
42 Russell Street
Melbourne, Victoria, Australia 3000

Church of Scientology Perth
3rd Floor, Pastoral House
156 St. George's Terrace
Perth, West Australia 6000

Church of Scientology Sydney
201 Castlereagh Street
Sydney, New South Wales
Australia 2000

Church of Scientology New Zealand
New Imperial Buildings, 2nd Floor
44 Queen Street
Auckland 1, New Zealand

AFRICA

Church of Scientology in Zimbabwe
74 Abercorn Street
Bulawaya, Zimbabwe/Rhodesia

Church of Scientology South Africa
3rd Floor, Garmor House
127 Plein Street
Cape Town 8001, South Africa

Church of Scientology Durban
57 College Lane
Durban 4001, South Africa

Church of Scientology Johannesburg
Security Building, 2nd Floor
95 Commissioner Street
Johannesburg 2001, South Africa

Church of Scientology
Johannesburg North
207-210 Ivylink, 124 Ivy Road Weg
Norwood 2192
Johannesburg, South Africa

Church of Scientology Port Elizabeth
2 St. Christopher Place
27 Westbourne Road
Port Elizabeth 6001, South Africa

Church of Scientology South Africa
226 Central House
Central Street
Pretoria 0002, South Africa

Church of Scientology Salisbury
102 Barton House
Cnr. Stanley & Moffat Streets
Salisbury, Zimbabwe/Rhodesia

Scientology Celebrity Centres

Church of Scientology
Celebrity Centre of Ann Arbor
301 North Ingalls
Ann Arbor, Michigan 48104

Church of Scientology
Celebrity Centre Los Angeles
5930 Franklin Avenue
Hollywood, California 90028

Church of Scientology
Celebrity Centre Las Vegas
3430 East Tropicana, Suite 50
Las Vegas, Nevada 89121

Church of Scientology
Celebrity Centre Paris
41, rue de la Tour d'Auvergne
75009 Paris, France

Other Organizations

COLOMBIA

Centro Cultural de Dianetica
Carrera 13 No. 90-36
Apartado Aereo 92419
Bogota, D.E. Colombia

MEXICO

Asociación Cultural Dianetica, A.C.
Hermes No. 46
Colonia Crédito Constructor
03940 México 19, D.F.

Instituto de Filosofia Aplicada, A.C.
Havre Numero 32
Colonia Juarez
06600 México 6, D.F.

Instituto de Filosofia Aplicada, A.C.
Plaza Rio de Janeiro 52
Colonia Roma
06700 México 7, D.F.

Organizacion Desarrollo
y Dianetica, A.C.
Providencia 1000
Conolia Del Valle
03100 México 12, D.F.

Centro de Dianetica de Polanco, A.C.
Mariano Escobedo 524
Colonia Anzures
11590 México D.F.

Instituto Tecnologico
de Dianetica, A.C.
Circunvalacion Poniente 150
Zona Azul Cuidad Satelite
53100 Estado de México, México

VENEZUELA

Asociación Cultural
de Dianetica, A.C.
Calle 150 No. 100-223
Apartado Postal 711
Valencia, Venezuela

GREECE

Hubbard Dianetics Institute
Ippokratous Street 175B
Athens, Greece

ISRAEL

Scientology Israel
Scientology "Shalom" Center
6 Frishman Street
Tel Aviv 63 578, Israel

ITALY

Dianetics Institute Brescia
Via Gorizia 12
26100 Brescia, Italy

Dianetics Institute di Milano
Galleria del Corso 4
20122 Milano, Italy

Dianetics Institute Novara
Corso Italia 42
28100 Novara, Italy

Associazione di Dianetics
e Scientology Padova
Via Pietro d'Abano 1
35100 Padova, Italy

Associazione di Dianetics
e Scientology Pordenone
Viale Martelli 4
33170 Pordenone, Italy

Associazione di Dianetics
e Scientology Roma
Via Francesco Carrara 24
00100 Roma, Italy

Dianetics Institute Torino
Piazza Statuto 12
10122 Torino, Italy

Associazione di Dianetics
e Scientology Verona
Via Leoncino 36
37121 Verona, Italy

PORTUGAL

Instituto de Dianetica Lisboa
Travessa Da Trindade 12-4
1200 Lisboa, Portugal

SPAIN

Asociación C. de Dianetica
Calle Puertaferrisa 17 (2nd Floor)
Barcelona 2, Spain

Asociación civil de Dianetica
Montera 20
Madrid 14, Spain

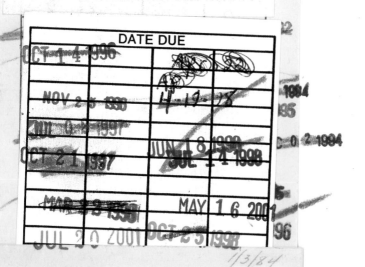